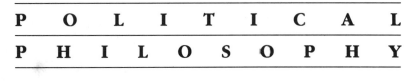

POLITICAL PHILOSOPHY

1

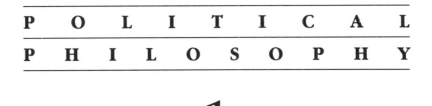

POLITICAL
PHILOSOPHY

1

Rights—
the New Quarrel
between the Ancients
and the Moderns

LUC FERRY
Translated by Franklin Philip

THE UNIVERSITY OF CHICAGO PRESS • CHICAGO AND LONDON

Luc Ferry is a professor at the Sorbonne and the
University of Caen.

The University of Chicago Press, Chicago 60637
The University of Chicago Press, Ltd., London

© 1990 by The University of Chicago
All rights reserved. Published 1990
Printed in the United States of America

99 98 97 96 95 94 93 92 91 90   5 4 3 2 1

Originally published in Paris as
*Philosophie politique 1. Le Droit:
la nouvelle querelle des Anciens et des Modernes.*
© Presses Universitaires de France, 1984.

Library of Congress Cataloging-in-Publication Data

Ferry, Luc.
 [Droit. English]
 Rights : the new quarrel between the Ancients and the Moderns / Luc Ferry ; trans-
lated by Franklin Philip.
  p.   cm.—(Political philosophy : 1)
 Translation of: Le droit.
 ISBN 0-226-24471-7 (alk. paper)
 1. History—Philosophy.   2. Historicism.   I. Title.   II. Series:
Ferry, Luc. Philosophie politique. English ; 1.
D16.8.F45213   1990
901—dc20   89-20335
                                                                            CIP

⊗ The paper used in this publication meets the minimum requirements
of the American National Standard for Information Sciences—Permanence
of Paper for Printed Library Materials,
ANSI Z39.48-1984.

CONTENTS

v

ABBREVIATIONS

LH   Alexis Philonenko. *La Liberté humaine dans la philosophie de Fichte*. Paris: Vrin, 1966.

ND   Theodor W. Adorno. *Negative Dialectics*. Translated by E. B. Ashton. New York: Seabury Press, 1983.

NR   Leo Strauss, *Natural Right and History*. Chicago: University of Chicago Press, 1953.

"OM"   Martin Heidegger. "Overcoming Metaphysics." In *The End of Philosophy,* translated by Joan Stambaugh. New York: Harper and Row, 1970.

"PP"   Leo Strauss. "What is Political Philosophy?" In *Political Philosophy: Six Essays by Leo Strauss,* edited by Hilail Gildin. Indianapolis: Pegasus/Bobbs Merrill, 1975.

SK   Johann Gottlieb Fichte. *Foundations of the Entire Science of Knowledge*. Translated by Peter Heath and John Lachs. New York: Appleton Century-Crofts, 1970.

SR   Johann Gottlieb Fichte. *The Science of Rights*. Translated by A. E. Kroeger. New York: Harper and Row, 1970.

ST   Martin Heidegger. *Schelling's Treatise on the Essence of Human Freedom*. Translated by Joan Stambaugh. Athens: Ohio University Press, 1985.

"TW"   Leo Strauss. "The Three Waves of Philosophy." In *Political Philosophy: Six Essays by Leo Strauss.*

US   Friedrich von Schelling. *On University Studies*. Translated by E. S. Morgan. Athens: Ohio University Press, 1966.

"WP"   Martin Heidegger. "The Age of the World Picture." In *"The Question Concerning Technology" and Other Essays,* translated by William Lovitt. New York: Garland, 1977.

INTRODUCTION

1. The Enlightenment in Question

Faced with instances of totalitarianism, contemporary thinkers seem, with rare exceptions,[1] to have given up on the ideals that animated the *philosophes* of the Enlightenment. Progress, emancipation through reason, "publicness" in the Enlightenment sense, are notions that now invite a smile and are even open to the "suspicion" of playing a role in the most calamitous episodes in human history. It is not unusual to read that totalitarianism is the effect of an unrestrained will to incarnate reason, or the universal, in the particular, as though reason must be suspected of violence, of tyranny with regard to the real—theories too widespread during the last decade for there to be a need here to identify their various formulators. From there, to declare, as the archbishop of Paris, Msgr. Lustiger, did recently in arguing the importance of the religious phenomenon in Poland, that "reason is also a gulag," it is but a short step that only the faint-hearted would fail to take.

The most remarkable thing, however, is that this rejection of reason appears so universal within philosophy that it has entered certain streams of thought that claimed, at least originally, to be Marxist. This is very clear, for example, in the Critical Theory of the Frankfurt School, whatever its initial wavering in regard to the ideal of socio-economic rationalization: Max Horkheimer's "Traditional and Critical Theory" of 1937 certainly still indicted irrationality in its description of a bourgeois economy that "is not governed by any plan [and] is not consciously directed to a goal of general interest".[2] Horkheimer was decrying any cleavage between reason and reality, and thus striving toward a rationalization of the social field—to the extent that accepting a gap between reason and reality in this domain would be "a sign of contemptible weakness . . . and to surrender to such weak-

1

ness is nonhuman and irrational."[3] In the first Critical Theory's conviction[4] that rationalization meant the emancipation of humanity through the avoidance of the dangers of self-interest, there was certainly an analysis of how reason in a bourgeois society could become the tool of such interests—but this "instrumental reason" was just an insufficiently self-critical version of reason, an accomplice of irrationality, so forgetful of its liberating function that it makes "a personal peace treaty between the philosopher and an inhuman world."[5] By contrast, a quite different understanding of the links between rationality and oppression appears in Horkheimer's final writings, with the formulation of what in 1970 he called "a new critical theory."[6]

For reasons too involved to recall here, Critical Theory, starting in the 1950s, derived oppression and inhumanity from rationality itself, as its inevitable extension. Totalitarianism henceforth appeared to flow naturally from progressive rationalization: "Today we see the society's future very differently from the way we were beginning to see it previously. We have reached the conclusion that society will evolve toward a totally administered world; that everything will be regulated, everything!"[7] in a certainly perfect actualization of social justice—the aim of reason—but also and indissolubly in a radical annihilation of all individual autonomy. And Horkheimer saw in the most visible totalitarianisms of the time, those of Hitler and Stalin, simple excesses in the process of total rationalization; "They tried to carry out a too-brutal unification, and exterminated all those who did not submit." The drift toward a society where "everything can be regulated automatically, be it the administration of the state, of traffic, or of consumption," remained ineluctable and "immanent in the evolution of humanity" toward a rationalization that, once achieved, will carry with it the death of the autonomous individual: for it is in *total* rationalization that rationality is totalitarian, and oppression is not the product of merely one face of reason (instrumental reason)—to be criticized by reason itself and to be transcended by further reason—but the product of reason itself.

Setting aside the question of how much Theodor Adorno's project for a "negative dialectics" proved to elicit doubt or to raise objections, I shall confine myself to noting that Horkheimer's and Adorno's thought—whatever its fate—was wary of any romantic escape from the modern era.

It is different for writings that, drawing their source and inspiration in Nietzsche's thought or in phenomenology, do not hesitate to link up, most often innocently or unconsciously, with the romantic themes most dear to the first critics of the Enlightenment: they are critical of rationalism, voluntarism, individualism, science and technology; and they value nature over artifice, society over the state, teleology over mechanism, and, in the final instance, ancient thought over modern thought.[8]

It is this attitude of "retreat" from modernity that I propose to analyze and discuss through one of its most original representatives, Leo Strauss. As the reader will note, the viewpoint adopted here is resolutely "modern"—which is not to say that it fails to appreciate the unshrinkable distance separating us from the eighteenth century. Taking a position in favor of the moderns—in favor of one particular idea of democratic rationality and equality—cannot be done naively, without going through intermediate steps, for example, on the manner of a "return" to the thought of Montesquieu, Kant, or Tocqueville. On the contrary, it should take full account of, and not ignore, the objections recently raised from the viewpoint of the ancients to democratic values, for these objections surely have a certain philosophical and historical legitimacy.

I choose to discuss Strauss's writings precisely because, of the various contemporary faces of this return to the ancients, his *political* critique of modernity seems to be fueled by assuredly the most radical and vigorous deconstruction of the *philosophical* presuppositions of this modernity: Heideggerian phenomenology.

To forestall any misunderstandings this comparison could engender, I must add that the comparison is in no way meant to blur the sometimes great differences between Strauss and Heidegger. Whatever Strauss's admiration for his former teacher at Marburg, whom along with Hannah Arendt he considered the indisputably greatest thinker of the twentieth century—much superior to Franz Rosenzweig![9]—Strauss was eventually to inveigh against Heidegger's attack on the Platonic dualism of the ideal and the real: unlike Heidegger, Strauss never gave up the idea that the critique of modern rationality was to lead not to any sort of irrationalism but to another form of reason (ancient reason), that "the very disavowal of reason must be reasonable disavowal" (*NR*, p. 36). In other words, Strauss was convinced—and this would have surely made Heidegger smile—not only that natural right was possible and indispensable for judging (evaluating) positive reality, but also that "there cannot be natural right if the fundamental problem of political philosophy cannot be solved in a final manner" (*NR*, p. 35).

And yet, however naive this statement as regards Heideggerianism, Strauss's critique of modernity drew its inspiration from the phenomenological deconstruction of metaphysical humanism, a deconstruction almost literally transposed to an area that admittedly Heidegger seemingly ignored: political philosophy. Like Heidegger, Strauss condemned not any particular feature of modernity but modern rationality as a whole. As with Heidegger, again, the modern era has tended to decline from the beginning. (It doesn't matter here whether we think of this decline as either the emergence of the domination of subjectivity and technology or the emergence of historicism and positivism.) In this view, all faces of modernity, even and especially the ones that apparently claim to counteract this decline, are in reality leading to it all the more certainly. Do Rousseau and Kant only seem to argue against British utilitarianism and thus to be applying a brake on the advent of historicism? In reality, they merely hastened its coming by leading to the emergence of Hegel's philosophy of history. Although this universe where everything converges in decline still contains some "bright spots" (Kant and Schelling for Heidegger, Spinoza for Strauss), that is merely because they hark back to Plato and Aristotle and thus are not in any way modern bright spots (hence their transience).

Because Heidegger's thought is still often misunderstood, even, for obvious reasons, suppressed (Heidegger belonged for eleven years to the Nazi party), it may be useful here to recall the great themes of his critique of modernity. We can then truly take the philosophical measure of the task of embracing, in a non-naive way, a modern humanism, a humanism that would have, as it were, integrated the objections made by the partisans of the ancients.

2. Heidegger's Critique of Modernity

It is usually said that Heidegger's thought is not political but confined to the history of philosophy. This claim, which has some truth in it, is nevertheless simplistic: no one now doubts that Heidegger's critique of modernity commits him to a phenomenology of domination, even totalitarianism. In his analysis of the "decline of the earth" during the reign of technology—a global decline seen as related to the decline of thought in the triumph of rational systematization— Heidegger's thinking leads to a prediction of the coming of the "totalitarian state" as a "necessary consequence" of the "development of technology."[10] The *Führers* who secure the powers of domination are the ever-present, although more or less dissimulating leaders in an age primarily devoted to organizing the technological exploitation of beings; for when the will to mastery and exploitation becomes the principle of all action, when everything must be subordinated to the attempt to guarantee the omnipotence of subject man and the assurance of his rule over beings, "men must be organized and equipped who serve leadership," men "who are the decisive suppliers who oversee all the sectors of the consumption of beings" ("OM," 105)—an assurance and guarantee that can be provided only by persons with a view of "the totality of beings and sectors" of exploitation and consumption; the will (peculiar to the technological era) to make indefinite use of beings as a whole requires this "ordering," this regulation and calculation of wear and tear without which everything would soon reduce to scarcity and which call for the relinquishment or delegation of powers to the *Führers* who control every area of social existence.

Totalitarianism then appears as a specifically modern phenomenon: it is part of "the essential configuration" of our time and is based on the domination of technology. According to Heidegger, in confronting totalitarianism, "moral outrage" ("OM," 105) stands at some distance from what is being thought of—i e., the domination of technology and its source. So we must go back from what is the "obvious manifestation"—the rule of the technicians/technocrats—to the "ground" from which it proceeded: modern metaphysics, meaning the rule of the subject who has become a "master and owner of nature," armed with the principle of reason which he imposes on all beings, and which is merely the philosophical version of the technical inquisition of the world. The main characteristics of domination in the modern era—rationality of system (where each "being" is explained), a metaphysics of subjectivity (where the subject is the ground and model for every being), the global domination of technology (where man is master and owner of nature), and economic and socio-political totalitarianism (by which the wear and tear of beings is calculated and bureaucratically organized to be infinite)—are thought by Heidegger as four aspects of the same event, the same modernity. In other words, behind the *Führers* and the "total mobilization" that they ensure,[11] we must learn to see technicians, and behind the technicians, metaphysicians, understanding technology "in such an essential way that its meaning coincides with the term 'completed metaphysics'" ("OM," 93), in short, to the very essence of modernity.

This is the path we must follow in order to grasp (1) what for

Heidegger the true essence of modernity is, (2) the reasons why this modernity may be considered "declining," and consequently (3) what should prompt a return to classical thought so we may discover the signs of a "new beginning."

The Essence of Modernity

"The fundamental event of the modern age is the conquest of the world as a picture" ("WP," 134). "In the great age of the Greeks," and even in medieval Christendom, "it would have been impossible to have anything like a world picture" ("WP," 133). Modernity as such came along only "when the world became picture," which happened "as soon as man brought his life as *subiectum* into precedence over other centers of relationship" ("WP," 134).

These three propositions constitute Heidegger's basic thinking about modernity. To grasp their import, we need to spell out their metaphysical significance. For we can place Heidegger's ideas about modernity by starting with a certain consideration of what it is "to be in being" and a particular concept of truth, both originating with Descartes.

In brief, the metaphysical essence of modern times lies in the definition of being as "objectiveness of representing" and of truth as "the certainty of representation" ("WP," 127). Beginning with Descartes, "what is, in its entirety, is . . . taken in such a way that it first is in being only insofar as it is set up by man, who represents and sets forth [*durch den vorstellenden-herstellenden Menschen gestellt ist*]" ("WP," 129–30; translation modified), and this is just what makes possible something like "a picture of the world." If there was no ancient or medieval picture of the world, if the idea of it is even absurd, the reason is, conversely, that medieval and ancient thought did not define being as what a representation presents to a subject.

In the Middle Ages, a being is a being not because it is "brought before man as the objective, in the fact that it is placed in the realm of man's knowing and of his having disposal," but because it is *ens creatum,* created by "the personal Creator-God acting as the highest cause" ("WP," 130). The medieval definition of being—the medieval ontology, if you will—was done through analogy: for a being to be a being it (1) had to belong to the order of created things, and (2) "as thus caused," had to correspond "to the cause of creation (*analogia entis*)" ("WP," 130).

The gulf separating modernity from the ontology of the Greeks is greater yet: in Greek ontology—insofar as we can interpret pre-

Socratic thought—being is not based on a theology, nor a fortiori is it measured by the yardstick of subjectivity: being does not get its being from its representability or visibility to man, so that it retains its share of obscurity (of invisibility) and of the mystery indissolubly inhering in the question, therefore left open, of its origin: "That which is does not come into being at all through the fact that man first looks upon it, in the sense of a representing that has the character of subjective perception. Rather, it is man who is looked upon by that which is" ("WP," 131; translation modified). The Greeks thus knew how to "harvest" and "save" phenomena without yielding to the metaphysical (i.e., idealist) temptation to reduce the ontological dimension of phenomena merely to being present to consciousness. The Greeks did not forget that component of "veiling" implied in any manifestation, so that a proposition like the one in which Berkeley summarized the idealist position on objectivity—*esse est percipi aut percipere*—would have been utterly foreign to them. Thus in Hellenism there can be no *Weltbild*, no image or global conception of the world, for the simple and valid reason that the totality can never be the object of vision. The Greek sense is not vision but hearing, so "Greek man is the hearer (*der Vernehmer*) of that which is, and this is why in the age of the Greeks the world cannot become a picture" ("WP," 130; translation modified).

In summary, the metaphysical basis of modernity lies in the assimilation of human subjectivity (of consciousness supplied with representation) to the Greek notion of *hypokeimenon,* a term that initially means "that-which-lies-before, which, as ground, gathers everything onto itself" ("WP," 128). In Greek the *hypokeimenon* does not designate human subjectivity but merely, in the etymological sense, the thing underlying the visible qualities, and translates as the Latin *subiectum.* In the Greek world and even in the Middle Ages, the *hypokeimenon* or *subiectum* has "no special relationship to man and none at all to the I," and it is only with the dawn of modern metaphysics in Descartes that "man becomes the primary and only real subiectum," i.e., "the relational center of that which is as such" ("WP," 128).

Interpreting Heidegger's thought freely, we could say that the positing of human subjectivity at the foundation and center of the world, by which modernity contrasts with the classical era, displays three outstanding facets of metaphysics, whose worldly actualization can take the form of totalitarianism:

1. The metaphysics of subjectivity is first spelled out as idealism

based on the principle of reason, a feature that culminated in the Hegelian system, which Heidegger believed "the pinnacle of metaphysics."[12] Because of the principle of reason—first formulated by Leibniz as *"nihil est sine ratione"*—the subject sees natural and historical reality as fully rational (explainable), at least in principle or by itself. This ontological side-taking (a "subjective" logical principle is transferred to being itself, for it is posited that being cannot be without corresponding fully to this principle) definitely leads to Hegelian idealism, for it presupposes, according to the hallowed formula, the perfect rationality of the real, i.e., the identity of the real and the rational. By applying this principle ontologically, man assures himself of a theoretical mastery over a world without mystery. Modern science, which is simply an appendage of metaphysics, can "have disposal over anything that is when it can either calculate it in its future course in advance or verify a calculation about it as past" ("WP," 126–27). The "calculation" (*ratio*) involved in explanation (*rationem dare*) then appears as the scholar's main activity, be he scientist or historian. Heidegger's whole critique of modern science—adopted by Hannah Arendt in connection with the historical sciences, notably in her article "Understanding and Politics,"[13]—consists in showing how its attempt (theoretically) to dominate the world merely reflects an implicit metaphysics still holding sway in it without its realizing it.

2. But viewing subjectivity as the center of a world represented as rational in the transparency of a potentially omniscient consciousness (we think of the rationalist philosophers of history) does not exhaust the whole of modernity's use of the notion of subjectivity. Heidegger stresses that the newness of the modern age

> in this event by no means consists in the fact that now the position of man in the midst of what is, is an entirely different one in contrast to that of medieval and ancient man. What is decisive is that man himself expressly takes up this position as one constituted by himself, that he *intentionally* maintains it as that taken up by himself. . . . There begins that way of being human which [means] the realm of human capability as a domain given over to measuring and executing, for the purpose of *gaining mastery* over that which is *as a whole.* ("WP," 132; emphasis added)

In other words, modern metaphysics is not just speculative and contemplative but also the vehicle for a practical and voluntarist plan to secure dominion over nature and history. Besides Descartes—the source of all these "facets" of subjectivity—the reference here is to Kant and Fichte, rather than to Hegel, insofar as their practical philos-

INTRODUCTION

ophy leads to the greatest development of the thesis that the essence
of subjectivity is the will, and the goal of human activity the transformation of the world. Rooted in this thesis, according to Heidegger, is
violence, even the Terror that inevitably accompanies the worldly actualization of metaphysics (Hannah Arendt largely subscribed to this
analysis, notably in her book *On Revolution*). The probably arguable
pertinence of this interpretation of modern ethics[14] matters little
here. At this point it is appropriate to stress that, despite the terroristic effects Heidegger thought this thesis was apt to produce, the will
is still subordinate to an end: if modern man applies himself not only
to producing an interpretation of the world (with Hegel) but also to
transforming it, he doubtless does so with the goal of securing his
happiness, even his freedom. The ethical will, however conceived,
remains a will to *something*.

3. This is not the case with the third and final facet of metaphysical subjectivity, which Heidegger illustrates by the Nietzschean
theory of "the will to power." Indeed, with the will to power—and
here again, I set aside the question of the "philological" accuracy of
Heidegger's analyses—, the human will ceases to concern an end
(happiness or freedom): it turns in on itself and becomes the "will to
will," a quest for power for the sake of power, or for power as such.
The worldly actualization of this ultimate or final facet of modern
metaphysics is obviously technology ("OM," sec. 10), or if you will,
"instrumental reason," since in this last facet the question of ends
cannot, by definition, be asked: the only thing that matters is the
Zweckrationalität in Weber's sense, the consideration of the means,
whatever the ends. "[T]he will to will absolutely denies every goal
and only admits goals as means" ("OM," 36). This final facet of metaphysical subjectivity has two main features: on the one hand, it constitutes a veritable *Aufhebung* (preserving transcendence) of two
first stages: reason and will. On the other hand, these two terms are
used only to ensure this subjectivity of "mastery for the sake of mastery": "The will to will forces the calculation and arrangement of
everything for itself as the basic form of appearance, only, however,
for the unconditionally protractible guarantee of itself" ("OM," 93).

Modernity in Question

Given this brief description of the essence of modernity, we are
left wondering what dangers Heidegger thinks modernity poses to
the fate of humanity. For, even if "moral outrage" is not in order, it
is evident that only by getting away from this modernity may we

9

see the need to revive the tradition of what Heidegger calls "the great age of the Greeks"—an era of thought in which man had "not yet" "brought his life as *subiectum* . . . at the center of every relation" ("WP," 135).

In the final structure of modern metaphysics, the will to will or technology, "man as *animal rationale,* here meant in the sense of the working being, must wander through the desert of the earth's desolation" ("OM," 85). By belonging to this structure, and to ensure its infinite perpetuation (which this structure by itself requires), man is condemned to organize unremitting production and consumption as versions of domination for the domination of being. This "decline occurs through the collapse of the world characterized by metaphysics, and at the same time through the desolation of the earth stemming from metaphysics" ("OM," 86)—a collapse and devastation that man, like someone running in order not to fall, inevitably brings about as a "laboring animal . . . left to the giddy whirl of its products" ("OM," 87). The putting of man in the position of beast of burden whose furthest horizon is "this rigidification"—in the sense in which Hannah Arendt, echoing Heidegger,[15] gives the term—"confirms the most extreme blindness to the oblivion of Being" ("OM," 86). "The supreme and most hidden anguish" (*Angst*) into which modernity plunges us may henceforth be expressed in a phrase: "The abandonment of Being" ("OM," 103).

To understand what Heidegger is getting at here, and to appreciate its consequences—which range from the "total" and unreserved domination of "banality" and *Sinnlosigkeit* (meaninglessness)[16] to "the 'world wars' with their character of totality" ("OM," 103)—we should recall how Heidegger means "finally to ask, once and for all,"[17] the question that modernity hides from view or, better, whose radical veiling forms the essence of modernity as decline, i.e., "the question of Being." Then and only then can we see how it behooves us not to "criticize" modernity (since Heidegger claims, perhaps unsuccessfully, to be wary of "moral outrage"), but at least to call it into question so as to get back to ancient thought.

Heidegger always insisted that, despite appearances, metaphysics had never before posed the question of Being, but immediately forgot it in favor of another question concerning "the being of beings," or the "beingness of beings." "From the beginning, in the history of Western thought, the being of beings was no doubt thought of," but "the truth of Being as Being remains unthought."[18] So we need to distinguish between the "directive question" of metaphysics, which addresses "the being of beings," and "the fundamental question"—never asked, according to Heidegger, before his own cogitation—which "uniquely" addresses Being as such: "The fundamental question about the essence and truth of Being ... is by no means equivalent to the traditional metaphysical question hitherto in use; the latter question is still asked only about beings, about what being is. It asks about the being of beings ... but it does not treat Being itself. The question about the being of beings is, certainly, the directive question of metaphysics, but it is not the fundamental question."[19] What are these two questions getting at, and how should we understand the expressions "being of beings" and "Being as Being"?

1. The directive question of metaphysics has two main features: "Metaphysics thinks of the Being of beings both in the ground-giving unity of what is most general, what is indifferently valid everywhere, and also in the unity of the all that accounts for the ground, that is, of the All-Highest."[20] To determine the vocabulary before explaining it, we will say that, under the first aspect, metaphysics is an "ontology" that gives the most general definition of what is common to every thing, what constitutes the "beingness" of every being, while, in its second aspect, metaphysics is a theology, a thought of the supreme being (God) as the basis of the whole of existence. We can now grasp the essential meaning of the directive question, and thus understand the significance of metaphysical activity.

As ontology, metaphysics produces a definition of being in general; in other words, it seeks and lists the criteria without which a thing could not be held to exist in reality. This, for example, was the task Plato set for himself when, anticipating modern metaphysics, he argued that the true criterion for the being of beings is stability, identity, or permanence—in short what he called the Idea (or Form) in contrast to the sensory which, because it is perpetually changing, contradictory, and contingent, cannot be credited with genuine being. This is again the goal in Descartes's *Meditations,* in the famous analysis of the lump of wax in which the philosopher attempts to isolate what is truly being, i.e., once again, what is permanent in stability beyond fluctuations in sensory qualities. (The wax is not truly hard or soft, colored or transparent, and so forth, for these qualities may vary depending on, say, the heat; therefore it is mere extended substance, susceptible of an infinite variety of shapes.) Another instance is the goal of Kant's theory of categories, in which a systematic picture is assembled of the aggregate of the characteristic features without which an object would not be an object. (A "something"

11

without quantity or cause, without a certain permanence beyond alterations over time, and the like, would not be an object.) The task of metaphysics as ontology is thus to interpret "the being of beings" (that in which a being is a being) in its most universal aspect.

But metaphysics has yet another dimension: that of theology: it "does not just consider being in its beingness, it considers at the same time being which, in purity, corresponds to beingness, the supreme being," [21] i.e., being that is both the most being (corresponding best to the definition of beingness) and the ground of all the other beings. The process by which metaphysics as ontotheology yields the idea of the supreme being, and posits its reality, may best be described by considering what Leibniz—the founder of modern ontotheology[22]—took to be the central question of metaphysics: "Why is there something rather than nothing?" [23] The very formulation of the question (the opening "why") inescapably indicates that the answer be specified by following the principle of sufficient reason or causality. The question, "Why is there something rather than nothing?" can only be answered by using the principle of reason (*Grund*), by searching, from reason to reason (from cause to cause), for the supreme basis (*Grund*) of the world. Indeed, it is only once we are in possession of such a basis that we will have genuine answers, according to the principle of reason, to the question. Thus, the principle of reason naturally leads to the positing of an unconditioned, absolute basis, i.e., a cause of the world that is not in turn the effect of another cause: God as cause of himself: "the Being of beings is represented fundamentally, in the sense of the ground, only as causa sui. This is the metaphysical concept of God." [24] It is in this very answer, guided by the principle of reason, that metaphysics misses the fundamental question, the question of Being; for where metaphysics "in the traditional way . . . is still inquiring on the causal plane by following the guiding thread of the 'why?,' the thought thinking of Being is totally denied in favor of the knowledge through representation of being born of being." [25] Therefore the metaphysical answer to the question of the origin of being does not reach Being, but only the supreme being, God. It will be possible for us, *a contrario,* to understand what Heidegger meant by the "fundamental" question of Being as such.

2. To grasp what this question is getting at—and thus what non-Being is—we should recall what Heidegger means by the expression "ontological difference." Ontological difference is the difference between Being and beings. This difference cannot be represented or

described as a thing. We may, however, situate it logically in relation to the question, "Why is there something rather than nothing?" If I say, "There is something," for example, "there is a table or a tree," the tree and the table (the something) are being: they are what is present for me in my representation. But when I am wondering about the "there is," I am wondering about Being as such. In an essentially inadequate but still meaningful formulation, we could say that Being is precisely the "there is," the very fact of the existence or presence of a being, to the extent that this fact is different from this presence itself. In other words, Being "is" the share of mystery inhering in any presence, the question mark in this presence that might just as well not be. Hence, causal thought is in essence forgetful of Being: in its theological answer to the question "why is there something rather than nothing?" metaphysics must dismiss this mystery; because of the principle of reason, it links the totality of being to a self-grounded basis (God), so that within this totality everything is rational (based on reason). Let there be being, and there you cease asking questions, for it is an ultimate reason for this existence. From the viewpoint of metaphysics, what Heidegger designates as Being can only appear as a void, because, for metaphysics, outside the totality of being, there is, strictly speaking, nothing. From the viewpoint of thinking that "leaves" metaphysics, on the other hand, this "nothing ... is originally the same as Being,"[26] for questioning Being (the mystery of "there is") is already to be thinking of the Other than Being (non-Being, which is to say, the void), which Heidegger can express in these terms: "Being—a question, but not a being."[27] Applied to history, metaphysical (equivalent to causal) thought must, from Heidegger's viewpoint and one also adopted by Hannah Arendt,[28] fail to determine the true essence of historicity: the uncanny and inexplicable looming up of the new (which Arendt analyzed in the ideas of revolution and action): "The unique, the rare, the simple—in short, the great, is never self-evident and hence remains inexplicable," which scientific historical (i.e., metaphysical) research cannot grasp as long as it "projects and objectifies the past in the sense of an explicable and surveyable nexus of actions and consequences" ("WP," 123).

We have seen how the "anguish" into which Heidegger sees modern times plunging us lies essentially in the extreme abandonment of Being characteristic of the final stage of metaphysics as the (technological) will-to-will.

We can now grasp the true origin of this "anguish"; it involves the very essence of modern metaphysics of which "the forgetfulness of Being" is a constituent—forgetfulness of Being, i.e., forgetful of the ontological difference, for the theological side of metaphysics leads to a view of the world with no room for mystery, for wonder: "The oblivion [forgetfulness] of Being is oblivion of the distinction between Being and beings. . . . The oblivion of the distinction . . . is the advent of metaphysics."[29] Attending to the supreme being, onto-theology does not notice that "the emptiness of Being can never be filled up by the fullness of beings, especially when this emptiness can never be experienced as such" ("OM," 107). Simply as an ontology, however, metaphysics forgets Being, for, defining the being of being as a presence for a subject (in representation), it overlooks the dimension of absence in every presence: this is the meaning of the metaphor of the "cube" running through the whole phenomenological tradition up to Merleau-Ponty: the perception of a cube always has a veiled or nonvisible dimension, a sixth and hidden face, and it is this sixth face that is, so to speak, the metaphor of Being, the portion of mystery, invisibility, at the core of everything visible.

Resolutely stationing themselves in the structure of metaphysics, science and modern technology are utterly incapable, despite what they may claim, of calling metaphysics into question. Moreover—and this is especially true, according to Heidegger, in the social sciences—by attacking the "abstraction" characteristic of metaphysical discourse (in contrast to the "concrete realism" of science), science and technology merely further mask the question of Being, since they do not even reach the question of the being of being. The sciences thus accept, being unable to call into question, a metaphysical definition of beingness: as the presence of what is calculable and manipulable by and for the subject, a definition that progressively becomes radically implicit in them. With modern times, "the collapse of philosophy becomes glaring; for it emigrates into logistics, psychology, and sociology"[30]—in short, into those disciplines Heidegger called "anthropology" because of the metaphysical structure on which they are grounded: "With the interpretation of man as *subiectum,* Descartes creates the metaphysical presupposition [for] future anthropology of every kind and tendency. In the rise of the anthropologies, Descartes celebrates his greatest triumph" ("WP," 140).

In this "age of the perfect absence of meaning,"[31] where "the unconditional uniformity of all kinds of humanity of the earth under the rule of the will to will makes clear the meaninglessness of human action which has been posited absolutely" ("OM," 110), there is seemingly no way out, the "domination of all the earth" appears to be the "necessary fate of the West" ("OM," 90). With man elevated to "the 'master' of what is 'elemental'" whose one and only goal is "a using up"—so that he "in truth has aimlessness as [his] aim"—, world wars become inevitable as a "variant of the using up of being" ("OM," 103–4). Now what it is that, in this unchecked course of domination, dashes every hope and justifies "the immense suffering which surrounds the earth" ("OM," 110), is that in modernity Heidegger sees political conflicts played out at a level where nothing essential can truly be called into question: the common basis of all modern political theory is indeed subjectivity taken in its metaphysical sense: therefore it matters little—at least with regard to the thought that locates the ultimate "anguish" in "the abandonment far from Being"—whether the aim of politics be liberal individualism or collectivism, for "only because and insofar as man has actually and essentially become subject is it consequently necessary to confront the explicit question: Is it as an 'I' confined to its own preferences and freed into its own arbitrary choosing or as the 'we' of society; is it as an individual or as a community . . . ?" ("WP," 132; translation modified). Thus the "positive struggle against individualism or for the community" ("WP," 133) not only remains on the other side of what is being thought (equivalent to Being), but its protagonists get additional motivation through a secret connivance. In the belief that it is striking a blow at liberal selfishness, collectivism merely charges subjectivity to its account: "Subjective egoism . . . can be canceled out through the insertion of the I into the we. Through this, subjectivity only gains in power. . . . In the planetary imperialism of technologically organized man, the subjectivism of man attains its acme, from which point it will descend to the level of organized uniformity and there firmly establish itself" ("WP," 152), i.e., (to use Adorno's terminology) the "administered world" is the inevitable and fatal future of humanity once it has entered into modernity, the vanishing point toward which all political activism converges beyond apparent conflicts that still create—for whoever does not grasp the essence of this modernity—the illusion, itself deeply modern, of things possible.

The Return to Antiquity: Hegel and Constant "Overturned"

The "task of thought"—which, under these conditions, can only be conceived in a elitist way, for authentic (i.e., unsubjective) meditation is "not necessary for all, nor is it to be accomplished or even found bearable by everyone" ("WP," 137)—must be the attempt to break "out of" metaphysics, thus getting outside this modernity that from first to last is its completion or "acme," the "obstacle that forbids man the original relation of Being to man's essence."[32]. It is in this quest for "another beginning" ("OM," 96). that Heidegger links up with the "dawning word"[33] of the thinkers of antiquity.

Without making a caricature of what must, despite everything, be called a "return to the Greeks," we may say that for Heidegger it represents a genuine reversal of what Hegel, on the philosophical level, and Benjamin Constant, on the political level, diagnosed as profoundly positive in world history.

From the viewpoint of modernity, whether we are speculative philosophers or political theorists, Greek thought is in all respects of the order of the "not yet": "On the horizon [from the viewpoint] of speculative idealism, Greek philosophy is at the 'not yet' stage in relation to accomplishment." To spell out the nature of this "not yet," it does seem that subjectivity does "not yet" occupy the central place which it gets with Descartes and which, on the political level, signals the arrival of individualism, of that freedom of the moderns celebrated by Constant. For Hegel, "in the Greek world, the mind certainly enters for the first time in its free confrontation with Being," meaning Greece was the birthplace of philosophy as ontology, "but the Mind does not yet explicitly achieve absolute certainty of itself as subject knowing itself." We are not surprised, then, when Heidegger agrees with Hegel in seeing in Cartesianism the true birth of modernity, Heidegger uncovering the launching of the extreme forgetfulness of Being, Hegel, on the other hand, hailing the arrival of philosophy in its "homeland," since with Descartes "we in fact enter into an independent philosophy. . . . Here, we may say, we are at home; like the sailor at the end of his long voyage on the stormy seas, we may cry 'Land!' "[36]

It is then striking to note how similarly Hegel and Heidegger judge Greece in relation to modernity (save that, obviously, the evaluative signs are reversed): Greece is the absence of subjectivity; with Descartes, "the subject/object relation appears in its full light. . . . On the other hand, all pre-Cartesian philosophy was limited to a pure representation of the objective. Even the soul and the mind are represented on the model of the object,"[37] so that Hegel sees the ancient Greek as not yet subject, or, more exactly, as subject "in himself," but not "for himself," for he has "not yet returned in himself as in our day."[38] Where Hegel takes this "not yet" to indicate a lack, a deficiency inherent in an idea that had not evolved, Heidegger sees the sign of a genuine resistance to this ineluctable decline of metaphysics toward a radical forgetfulness "of what is the most worthy of question": "to our minds, Greek philosophy appears no less in a 'not yet.' But it is the 'not yet' of the unthought, not a 'not yet' that satisfies us, but a 'not yet' that *we* do not satisfy and are far from satisfying."[39]

How are we to understand this "not yet" which is seen as a sign of our own inadequacy, and thereby presents a challenge to the idea of "progress" inevitably conveyed by the modern, rationalist philosophy of history (and it is on this precise point that Strauss's thinking will come in)?

The task of the thought that "in every sense 'leaves' metaphysics"[40] and that in this progression links up with Hellenism may be succinctly stated: escaping this extreme "anguish" "involves putting thought back into the presence of the forgetfulness of Being,"[41] i.e., "in the presence" of Being as this "withdrawal," the "there is" that is forever inaccessible to the view of the subject whose thought is limited to the representation of present beings; and it is on this point that Heidegger encounters the Greek idea of the truth as *aletheia*. In modernity the truth is invariably defined as *adaequatio rei ad intellectum:* "The true, whether it be a matter or a proposition, is what accords, the accordant [*das Stimmende.*]"[42] This definition of truth is obviously not neutral: it presupposes a certain ontology, a certain definition of the being of beings as presence (stability, identity, permanence) for a subject in its representation. To speak the truth is to face, in vision, this present (adequacy).

The Greek word *aletheia*—which Heidegger translates as "unveiling" or "unhousing"—points (by the privative prefix "*a*—" toward the dimension of invisibility or mystery that is the innermost depth of every presence[43]—in short, toward Being as withdrawal. For someone who thinks starting from subjectivity and thus reduces the totality of being to presence, it is forever impossible to grasp the essence of *aletheia* and thus the essence of Hellenism, if "*aletheia,* the unhousing, is not in play merely in the fundamental words of Greek thought" but "in the whole of the Greek language, which speaks differently, when we hear it, when we leave aside . . . modern representations . . . and when we are seeking in the Greek world neither personalities nor consciousness."[44] We are not surprised, then, if Hegel, the prototype of modern man, "cannot . . . detach being in the Greek sense of *einai* from the relation to the subject and deliver it from his own essence."[45]

From this anti-Hegelian and thus antimodern viewpoint, Heidegger traces[46] the intellectual history of the break that, with Galileo and Descartes, marked the advent of modern science and the forgetting of the Aristotelian *episteme,* an often masterful analysis of this shift that goes, in Koyré's beautiful phrasing, "from the closed world to the infinite universe."

It would clearly be out of place to follow Heidegger's analysis. Instead, I shall merely indicate how the essential points of rupture between the Greek and the modern conceptions of nature opened the way (and that is truly the least one can say) for Strauss's ideas about natural right: in showing how in the Greek sense nature is a substantial, hierarchical order (cosmos) that is meaningful in itself and not inert raw material that can receive meaning only from the actions of a human subject, Heidegger creates the possibility of a return to the political philosophy of the Greeks as a philosophy of nonsubjectivity in which nature is normative (each creature should find its place in the cosmos as a function of its nature and not as a function of a subjective norm of reason), and the social order is no less naturally hierarchical. The reader trying to understand the strictly cosmological bases of this representation of a universe whose ordering owes nothing to subjectivity, unlike the great modern philosophical systems, is referred to Heidegger's lucid commentaries on Aristotelian physics.[47]

It seems to me more important, in elucidating the philosophical and political stakes in this new quarrel between the ancients and the moderns, to retrace the main currents of its purely philosophical logic, for two reasons whose significance I think is too little appreciated, probably owing to the compartmentalization between disciplines:

- First, it is clear—and this is simply an observation—that this philosophical logic is not explicit in Heidegger's students, notably those who, like Strauss or Arendt, opted to carry on this "new quarrel" at the political level, hence in a field other than speculative philosophy. Whatever the differences between Strauss and Heidegger, it is undeniable—for someone who can momentarily shelve his biases—that on the purely philosophical level, the logic of a return to the Greeks proceeds from the same inspiration. Reconstructing this philosophical logic will help us locate the discussion of Strauss's theses at the only level where they may be justifiable (which does not mean that Strauss's thinking "reduces" to an "application" of Heidegger's ideas to political philosophy, or that its only source is Heidegger's philosophy).

- Clearly, Strauss's critique of historicism was modeled on Heidegger's deconstruction of modernity as the imperialism of subjectivity, for with the advent of subjectivity (1) man loses the chance to refer to a "transcendent standard" (a natural, nonsubjective law) for condemning positivity, and (2) he is inevitably cast, as the will-to-will, into a unchecked mobility to which no ultimate purpose can be assigned, i.e., absolute historicism[48]— or into what Arendt called ideology.[49]

Thus, by positioning myself at this level, I would like to conclude this introduction with a consideration of the philosophical and political significance of this logic of a return to the ancients.

3. New Quarrel, Phony Quarrel, or Bad Quarrel?

First, to get straight to the point and incur the risk of appearing naive (since it is not presently customary to bedevil oneself about the truth of some philosophy), I shall indicate what seems to me correct and possibly fruitful in this critique of modernity.

- In the first place, the criticism of modern metaphysics as idealism seems to me clearly incontrovertible, even if, as I have suggested elsewhere, it appears unoriginal and most likely less profound in comparison with Kant's critique.[50] Nevertheless, any philosophical project explicitly subscribing to modernity cannot afford to ignore this deconstruction, the problem being to show how this deconstruction does not, however, ineluctably lead to a return to the ancients.
- The rejection of historicism—"historicism" meaning the denial, in favor of historical process, of any dimension of transcendence—seems to me a genuine prerequisite to any political philosophy, even to any critical philosophy worthy of the name. Here again, someone who claims to be a modernist must face the major difficulty of showing how subjectivity is not inevitably synonymous with historicism.

Accounting for these two principles—the denial of both idealism and historicism—brings us to the central question of this book: how can we argue for a modern humanism that is neither naively metaphysical nor flatly historicist, and that makes possible a modern political philosophy?

For, once we have identified the prerequisites that Heidegger's or Strauss's critique of modernity imposes on this project, we still have to point out the risks inherent in this critique and to indicate how they prohibit assent. These risks seem to me of two kinds: political and philosophical.

The Political Risks of the Return to the Ancients

The political motivation for a return to classical thinking is deeply antidemocratic. Given that democracy seems not incompatible with Hellenism, since democracy found its first adherents in ancient Greece, I should make clear what I mean by "antidemocratic." First, classical political philosophy (in Strauss's sense), insofar as it assumed that politics is an imitation of the natural order, was inegalitarian: the Greek universe—in both its cosmology and politics—was naturally hierarchical: just as "'above' is not anything you like, but where fire, and what is light move [to]. Likewise, 'below' is not anything you like, but where heavy and earth-like things move [to]," and "every place should have 'above' and 'below,' and . . . each body should naturally move to and remain in its proper places, and this it must do either above or below,"[51] individuals are similarly and naturally—i.e., irreversibly—destined to occupy different hierarchical stations in the social body—of which Plato's *Republic* is the most striking example. Apart from such a cosmology, Greek slavery is unthinkable; on the basis of such a cosmology, slavery is defensible. This obviously does not mean that the modern political world—and here I am thinking of liberalism—is truly egalitarian. It does tend to be so, however, and here Tocqueville's analysis has lost none of its acuity, and its persistent inequalities are not seen as natural (in the Greek sense) or de jure, but as de facto inequalities of talent or merit. Even in the least "democratic" liberal thought, an individual may conceivably change his condition; for example, in a system where property-owning suffrage prevails, he succeeds in becoming an "active citizen." In classical natural right, this mobility is unthinkable, for there inequality is a matter of cosmic nature. In this sense, one cannot without absurdity be a Straussian and a liberal, a partisan of both the ancients and moderns. This danger was spotted by Hannah Arendt—whose sympathies for modernity were more than mixed—when she ridiculed some of Strauss's political stands, as Elisabeth Young-Bruehl reports in her monumental biography of Arendt: "Strauss was haunted by the rather cruel way in which Hannah Arendt had judged his assessment of National Socialism: she had pointed out the irony of the fact that a political party advocating views Strauss appreciated could have no place for a Jew like him."[52] The humor is indeed cruel, perhaps even tasteless, but it hits home on one score: the neoconservative tendency to sacralize natural inequalities, even to inscribe them, in fact and in law within the social and political hierarchy.

"Phenomenological" critiques of modernity have a second aspect that also seems to me to run counter to democratic thought: for, as the writings of Michel Villey have shown, the Greek universe clearly had no place for what are now called human rights. In the Greek conception—which is still operative in Roman law—the law (le droit)[53] cannot be thought a norm of conduct: the law is, as it were, merely society's medicine which reestablishes order, putting each person in his place when this cosmic order, like a diseased organ, is disturbed. In this regard, we may read Strauss's major work, Natural Right and History, as one of the most vigorous critiques of the very idea of human rights—a critique that falls into the line of that phenomenological deconstruction of a modernity conceived, according to a formula Strauss borrowed from Nietzsche, as "human, all too human." The critics of modernity then find themselves in an acutely ironic situation when they claim to be attacking totalitarianism: after analyzing the plan for absolute mastery of the social, they condemn the will to transparency that leads to the inevitable terroristic goal of suppressing all social division; but once they have performed this "deconstruction"—analogous at every point to the one conducted against metaphysics—, they remain resolutely unable, precisely because of the critique of subjectivity on which they based their critique of totalitarianism, to think of something like human rights[54]—an inability that writers like Strauss or even Arendt make no effort to conceal; witness, for example, the chapters on human rights in Arendt's Origins of Totalitarianism, where she harks back, certainly with nostalgia, but nonetheless with resolution, to the thinking of Edmund Burke.

By indicating the political "risks" of a return to the ancients—naturalistic inegalitarianism and the rejection of human rights—, I am not seeking to discredit it philosophically but merely to point out its inevitable consequences: indeed, nothing would be more absurd than to pit the ancients against the moderns for the needs of a particular cause—criticizing revolutionary terrorism as the tyranny of subjectivity, or totalitarianism as the worldly actualization of metaphysics, and to treat oneself to the luxury of a good humanist conscience by championing Solidarity in Poland or denouncing General Pinochet in Chile! Here writers like Leo Strauss or Michel Villey have the very rare merit of coherence: human rights are a purely modern invention, bound up with the introduction of subjectivity as a foundation, and we find not the least trace of them in the Greek world. This coherence and rigor must be taken into account by anyone who, while criticizing the metaphysics of subjectivity, still believes in democracy and human rights and thus is wary of a "return to the Greeks."

The Philosophical Risks of Critiques of Subjectivity

If, as we have seen, the two basic "faces" of modern metaphysics are reason (the principle of reason) and free will (the ability to act in accordance to the representation of ends), the phenomenological deconstructions of modernity run two risks, which they do indeed incur in their less coherent versions—the risks of irrationalism and amoralism. I shall confine myself to a brief description of them since their analysis is pursued in the succeeding volume.[55]

—First, it seems to me undeniable that the radical critique of the principle of reason involves its practitioners in insurmountable aporias: to dare to write, as did Arendt subsequent to Heidegger, that any use of the principle of causality in the historical sciences leads the historian to repudiate "in fact the very object of his own science"[56] is not only to make an impossible wager (who can think more than a few minutes without using the principle of reason?) but also to commit a major philosophical error: the error of identifying any use of the principle of reason with ontotheology. Certainly, and I myself have insisted here that Heidegger's analysis is correct, it is thanks to the principle of reason that, going back from cause to cause, we reach the idea of a cause of the world that is cause of itself (which is equivalent to God). From there to conclude, however, that the principle of reason unfailingly drags us into this tangle, there is one step that cannot be taken without committing the patent absurdity of ranking the whole of scientific discourse with ontotheology. So it seems to me more reasonable—and less simplistic—to seek to limit this principle (rather than destroying it), i.e., to give it a critical status[57] (a principle of *method* enabling us to make sense of the world, and not a principle of ontology).

—It next seems to me that the criticism of the modern idea of

22

freedom, conceived as the faculty of acting spontaneously according the representation of ends (the will), also runs into insurmountable difficulties. Certainly, here again, the criticism is not baseless: it seeks to save the "miraculous," or, to put it less emphatically, the unpredictable character of action. To infer from this that the very idea of will is in essence "forgetfulness of Being"—since it amounts to thinking of the event as based on the voluntary consciousness of the subject, and not as *Ereignis,* a prompting of Being itself—, once again there is a step that cannot be taken without absurdity: for if it is Being that "acts" through us, if under these conditions it behooves us "to do nothing, merely to wait"[58] and to adopt the pure and simple attitude of "releasement" (*Gelassenheit*), any ethical view of the world, every form of criticism should vanish. It would be pointless, then, to clutter up the marketplace with books denouncing the ravages of technology, the horrors of totalitarianism, or "the banality of evil," because for someone thinking philosophically, "coherence," however conceived, cannot be a vain word. So we should perhaps learn to make a methodical and critical use of freedom, analogous to that of the principle of reason, i.e., not as an ontological truth, but as a regulative idea or horizon of meaning (sense).[59]

The new quarrel between the ancients and the moderns thus seems to me to be—and this is the suspicion with which this book originated—a bad quarrel. Furthermore, it may be a phony quarrel: for, on closer examination—I want to say: not to read the history of philosophy, "from Parmenides to Nietzsche," as though we were viewing a huge game of snakes and ladders in which the critic of modernity would obviously make the final move—is there not some naïveté, even paradoxically some historicism, in thinking that the ancients and the moderns are separate and succeed each other like "before" and "after"? How can we not be struck, for example, by the fact that Heidegger's divisions—and also Strauss's and Arendt's—of the history of speculative or political philosophy reproduce virtually unmodified the great stages in Hegel's philosophy of the history of philosophy: the Greeks (not yet subjectivity); the Middle Ages (still no subjectivity, but the emergence of the already premodern figure of the divine); Descartes, Galileo, Machiavelli, Vico—the triumphant looming up of subjectivity in the field of the philosophy of history! Only the signs of the value judgments are reversed, but the beautiful linear chronology is untouched, as profoundly logical in Hegel as in Strauss, for whom the sequence of the "three waves of modernity" is no less ineluctable than is, for Hegel, the transition from Descartes to Kant or from Kant to Schelling! And how are we to maintain that beautiful linearity, the unrelenting chrono*logy*, when we see among the moderns philosophers who are less modern than others, those who "almost" belong with the ancients (Kant and Schelling for Heidegger, Spinoza for Strauss), or among the ancients the oddly premodern (the Stoics or the Epicureans, for example, who are not, as we know, "true Greeks" by reason of the subjectivity that is forever tragically breaking through in their philosophy).

Lest I be misunderstood: in no way do I mean to cast doubt on the difference between what may be designated by the terms "antiquity" and "modernity." Aristotle's cosmology is plainly not that of Descartes. I would like merely to suggest that it might be philosophically fruitful to think of this opposition of the ancient and the modern not as a flatly chronological opposition (or "profoundly" historical which to my mind, makes no difference in this case) but as the structural opposition between two ideal types, each of which is no doubt more fully embodied in one epoch than in another, but which still always constitute possible expressions of human thought. In this and only this sense could we understand that from Aristotle to Descartes there is perhaps neither progress (Hegel) or decline (Strauss, Heidegger), but merely the thematization of ontological structures that somehow remain possibilities for humanity as a whole. The quarrel between the ancients and the moderns could, even today, have some significance: conceived as structural, the opposition of the ancient and the modern may be indeed the stakes of a dialogue; conceived as chronological, the opposition leads ineluctably to an insurmountable division—in my opinion as unthinkable theoretically as it is ethically—of humanity: from Hegel's viewpoint, because the ancients are not yet fully men (they are so only "in itself" and not "for itself"); from Heidegger's and Strauss's viewpoint, because the moderns are no longer fully human, engaged as they are in a process of "reification" in which they lose their "authenticity" only to founder in "machine-ism" and animality.

Toward a Modern and Nonhistoricist Humanism

It is now easy to see the thesis of this book: if Heidegger's deconstruction of metaphysics and Strauss's critique of historicism are incontrovertible, and if, despite everything, we refuse to conclude that a "return to the ancients" is in order (because of the risks just mentioned), we must take up the challenge of showing how modernity may criticize itself and thus refrain from yielding to the wiles of metaphysics.

In other words, we must show how reason, free will, and equality (understood here in Tocqueville's sense, hence as the antithesis of the cosmic inequality of classical philosophy) may be conceived so that, by limiting themselves, they escape their metaphysical and historicist destiny.

In this investigation it seemed to me fruitful to inquire about Kant and Fichte's criticist problematic, whose posterity, through the Marburg School and the Frankfurt School, is still claimed by thinkers as otherwise different as Raymond Aron, Karl Popper, and Jürgen Habermas. To my knowledge, critical philosophy is indeed the only one in the history of modern philosophy to attempt to produce a rigorous criticism of metaphysics (which, as we shall see, also implies, before its time, a criticism of historicism) without, however, giving up reason, freedom, and equality—in short, what never existed in dogmatic metaphysics except in the form of unfulfilled promises.[60]

Fichte's thinking in particular, as it elaborated (without betraying) the spirit of Kant's criticism in the *Critique of Judgment,* seemed to me to allow for a genuine renewal of contemporary thought about the opposition between the ancients and the moderns, and perhaps even about contemporary political philosophy itself.

Literally rediscovered, thanks to the interpretation that Alexis Philonenko gives of Fichte's early writings,[61] Fichte's thought in my opinion has three main points of interest for us here:

- Starting with Kant's critique of metaphysics, Fichte's thinking is first presented as a systematic and in my opinion unrivaled deconstruction of the presuppositions of modern metaphysics. But this deconstruction, unlike Heidegger's, leads neither to romanticism—i.e., nostalgia for ancient Greece (seeing Fichte as a romantic is as absurd as viewing him as an idealist is fantastic)—nor to irrationalism: as in Kant, the metaphysical ideas retain, after the deconstruction that takes away all their truth, a certain use as regulative principles forming horizons of meaning or sense. (We shall be dwelling at some length on this particular status of the criticist critique of metaphysics.)
- On this score, Fichte's thought seems to me to contain the most powerful elements of a critique of the philosophical bases of historicism: for if we define historicism as the negation of the difference between reality and the ideal, and if rationalist (Leib-

nizian or Hegelian) metaphysics inevitably denies this difference and asserts the rationality of the real (hence, the identity of the real and the ideal), in modern philosophy it is assuredly criticist thought that wages the hardest battle, not only against the assimilation of the "is" and the "ought," of the *Sein* and the *Sollen,* but also against kinds of metaphysics of history that end in this assimilation.

- It is in this way that Fichte's philosophy may help us lay the foundations of both a philosophy of law and rights and a political philosophy that are both modern, i.e., valuing subjectivity and equality, and still nonhistoricist.

The comparison of the philosophical positions of Strauss and Fichte should thus enable us to make progress on the possibly central question of contemporary political philosophy: Is a nonmetaphysical humanism thinkable?

The Rejection of
Historicist Modernity:
Leo Strauss

Historicism and Positivism

Throughout his mature writings,[1] Leo Strauss endeavored to draw rigorous inferences from his analysis of the preconditions for political philosophy which he defined, echoing Plato, as "the attempt truly to know both the nature of political things and the right, or the good, political order."[2] For Strauss, political philosophy was indissolubly linked to the notion of "natural right," to the possibility of invoking, if only by way of questioning, a critical authority that transcended positive reality: "political life in all its forms necessarily points toward natural right as an inevitable problem. Awareness of this problem is not older than political science but coeval with it. Hence a political life that does not know of the idea of natural right is necessarily unaware of the possibility of political science and ... [conversely,] a political life that is aware of the possibility of science necessarily knows natural right as a problem" (*NR*, 81).

Thus, Strauss saw the negation of natural right—i.e., in the broadest sense, and whatever the aim of the idea of this natural right, the negation of the possibility of a "standard by which we can judge positive rights"—as the negation of all political philosophy (or science). More specifically, political philosophy, as thinking about natural right, could exist only on two conditions, or, if you will, on the basis of two minimum theoretical requirements, whose simplicity, as we shall see, is merely apparent:

1) First, for a political philosophy to be possible, we clearly need to recognize and admit the existence of a disparity between the real and the ideal, between the city as it is and the city as it ought to be. In the absence of such a

disparity, inquiry about the best form of political regime by definition makes no sense, for this disparity is what differentiates natural right from positive right.

2) The second condition is the possibility of a reasonable discussion of the best form of regime (the object of natural right), and of arriving at a true or plausible opinion on the subject. More generally, the domain of political values must not elude all reasonable dialogue.

According to Strauss, it is just these two conditions that the social sciences, the most recent incarnation of modernity, have set out to destroy, using two weapons against political philosophy, historicism and positivism: "Present-day social science rejects natural right on two different, although mostly combined grounds; it rejects it in the name of History and in the name of the distinction between Facts and Values" (*NR*, 4).[3]

—In the name of history is the first condition for denying the possibility of political philosophy, for any form of historicism leads to impugning the contrast between norm and fact. Here Strauss distinguishes three versions of historicism: (1) a "rationalistic" historicism whose chief representative is surely Hegel's philosophy of history which, culminating in the assertion of the rationality of the real, amounts to a denial of any chasm separating the ideal (the rational) from "positivity"; (2) an empiricist historicism, current in the humanities, which is intended to reveal the historical character of all thought and view of the world, including of course those claiming universality or eternity. "By denying the significance, if not the existence, of universal norms, the historical school destroyed the only solid basis of all efforts to transcend the actual" (*NR*, 15), and hence all efforts to transcend the "positive" in the name of the "natural"; and (3) an "existentialist" historicism—here Strauss is thinking essentially of Heidegger—which, although in a way radically different from the first two, also ends up eliminating the ideal/real pair which it criticizes as a metaphysical illusion originating in "Platonic dualism."

—Strauss saw "in the name of the difference between fact and value" a denial of the second precondition of political philosophy. This is the essence of positivism, which—though it acknowledges the existence of invariable principles not subject

PREAMBLE

to history—holds that the plurality, even the opposition, of these principles is a challenge to the very idea of rational choice.

Understood this way, positivism should not be confused with scientism (the idea that no question is unanswerable for science), but, on the other hand, it may be identified with the assertion that because the problems posed by "life" are inaccessible to scientific knowledge, they are not susceptible of any rational treatment and for that very reason are profoundly undecidable:[4] because the world of values is scientifically inaccessible, science must then confine itself to a neutral description of facts. So according to this version of positivism, there is no human authority that could rationally prove the superiority of one system of values over another. Now Strauss judged that "there cannot be natural right if human thought is not capable of acquiring genuine, universally valid, final knowledge within a limited sphere or genuine knowledge of specific subjects" (NR, 24). In this genuine "quarrel with positivism," which closely resembles the one between Theodor Adorno and Jürgen Habermas on one side and Karl Popper on the other, Strauss aimed at Hans Kelsen and especially Max Weber[5] in whose work he saw the most radical nonhistoricist denial of the notion of natural right: "It is the recognition of timeless values that distinguishes Weber's position most significantly from historicism. Not so much historicism as a peculiar notion of timeless values is the basis of his rejection of natural right. . . . He denied to man any science, empirical or rational, any knowledge, scientific or philosophic, of the true value system: the true value system does not exist; there is a variety of values which are of the same rank, whose demands conflict with one another, and whose conflict cannot be solved by human reason" (NR, 39, 41–42). Against this position, Strauss undertook to restore the view of the common consciousness, emphasizing even in its apparent flatness the feeling of impotence into which positivism plunges us in the face of what we all still recognize as unacceptable. It is in this sense, for example, that he does not hesitate to recall that "the biggest event of 1933 would rather seem to have proved, if such a proof was necessary, that man cannot abandon the question of the good society, and that he cannot free himself from the responsibility for an-

31

swering by deferring to History or to any other power different from his own reason" ("PP," 24).

Historicism and positivism seem to be the two preeminent characteristics by which the social sciences radically disallow political philosophy. Thus we cannot evade the question about how the social sciences came up with this negation, a rather mysterious process if we are to believe Strauss: "In the present state of our knowledge, it is difficult to say at what point in the modern development the decisive break occurred with the 'un-historical' approach that prevailed in all . . . philosophy" before the advent of historicism (*NR,* 13). Overall, however, the answer to this question is not in any doubt: it is the *whole* of modernity, not merely the modern social sciences, that must be called into question: "It was a predicament peculiar to eighteenth-century philosophy that led to the emergence of the historical school. The political philosophy of the eighteenth century was a doctrine of natural right. It consisted in a peculiar interpretation of natural right, namely, the specifically modern interpretation. Historicism is the ultimate outcome of the crisis of modern natural right" (*NR,* 34). The "Golden Age" of political philosophy is thus assigned a philosophical place: classical thought (meaning the ideas of the ancient Greeks); while, correspondingly, the historicist "decline," of which the social sciences represent merely only the most recent episode, originated with the modern theories of natural right; and the decline leading to this last phase of modernity extends over several "epochs," from Machiavelli to Nietzsche, along what Strauss calls "the three waves of modernity."

Allan Bloom (in an article described as the "text most illuminating and worthiest of its subject that one could read"[6]) summarizes Strauss's thought:

> [Strauss in *Natural Right and History*] could now present the classical meaning of nature and make plausible its use as a standard. Hence, he could see the intentions of the first modern philosophers who understood that view of nature and tried to provide a substitute for it. The later thinkers tried to resolve the difficulties inherent in the new view or to improve on it. Those difficulties, made manifest, led not to the return to the older view but to the abandonment of nature in favor of history, which in its first stage seemed to preserve reason and provide another standard, but which culminated in the rejection of reason and the disappearance

of any standard [Strauss] was always thinking of what he later called "the three waves of modernity": modern natural right, prepared by Machiavelli and developed by Bacon, Hobbes, Spinoza, Descartes, and Locke; the crisis of modern natural right and the emergence of history, begun by Rousseau and elaborated by Kant and Hegel; radical historicism, begun by Nietzsche and culminating in Heidegger.

Thus, in its aporetic attempt to find some equivalent to the Greek notion of "nature," all of modern philosophy inevitably conduces to historicism, forced by its abandonment of "nature" to substitute the concept of history, and then, for that of history, that of historicism. In this sense, modern political philosophy must be considered merely a process—no doubt progressive, but ineluctable—of the self-negation of political philosophy, so that an "adequate discussion of historicism would be identical with a critical analysis of modern philosophy in general."[7]

Strauss's argument thus takes the form of a syllogism that could be stated as follows:

- Major premise: Historicism and positivism are two radical negations of political philosophy.
- Minor premise: Since Machiavelli, modern philosophy has been throughout a process leading, despite appearances to the contrary (I shall come back to this point), toward this negation or, if you will, this self-suppression of political philosophy in favor of the philosophy of history.
- Conclusion: Because modernity is wholly historicist and positivist, the only chance for reconstructing a political philosophy lies in a return to ancient thought, to classical natural right.

I will say straightaway that this argument (admittedly simplified and somewhat schematically presented here, but, I believe, with no distortion of Strauss's thought) seems to me interesting in principle but unpersuasive in its conclusions: interesting in principle because it rightly accentuates the conflict between historicism and political philosophy, and thus clearly shows the need for any political thought to do some preliminary wondering about the philosophy of history: unpersuasive, however, for I doubt that modernity as a whole is historicist or prehistoricist. This claim assumes that, in the guise of plurality, modern philosophies of history reduce to unity and basically converge into univocally historicist thinking.

Objecting in principle to any external criticism[8] I shall not undertake here to show how modernity is the locus of a conflict between an irreducible plurality of philosophies of history.[9] So I shall attempt to follow Strauss's argument from within, even if that means noting occasional tensions or contradictions. I shall first analyze how Strauss sees modern political philosophy destroying itself in a historicist view of history, and how he sees this diagnosis as inevitably heralding a return to classical thought. Then, and then only, can we inquire about the possible limits of this critique of modernity and, later, about the appropriateness of a "restoration" of Hellenism.

"The Three Waves of Modernity": The Dissolution of Political Philosophy into Historicism

1. The Critique of Modern Natural Right

Strauss's critique of the whole of modern political philosophy presumes that we can detect the seeds of historicism not only in political ideas that are obviously and explicitly favorable to historicism but also in philosophies that appear to endorse the distinction between fact and right. Hence Strauss's thesis that modern philosophers since Machiavelli have—despite their more or less self-proclaimed will to get back to the authentic tradition of political philosophy—ironically hastened the emergence of their own historicist negation. This "phenomenology" of modernity lies at the core of "The Three Waves of Modernity":

> Modernity started from the dissatisfaction with the gulf between the is and the ought, the actual and the ideal; the solution suggested in the first wave was: to bring the ought nearer to the is by lowering the ought, by conceiving of the ought as not making too high demands on men, as being in agreement with man's most powerful and most common passion; in spite of this lowering, the fundamental difference between the is and the ought remained; even Hobbes could not simply deny the legitimacy of the appeal from the is, the established order, to the ought, the natural or moral law. Rousseau's concept of the general will which as such cannot err—which by merely being is what it ought to be—showed how the gulf between the is and the ought can be overcome. Strictly speaking, Rousseau showed this only under the condition that his doctrine of the general will, his political doctrine proper, is linked with his doctrine of the historical process, and this linking was the work of Rousseau's great successors, Kant and Hegel, rather than of Rousseau himself. According to this view, the rational or just society, the society characterized by the existence of a general will known to be the general will, i.e., the ideal is necessarily actualized by

the historical process without men's intending to actualize it. ("TW," 91).

There then appears the seemingly inevitable process that goes from Machiavelli's lowering of the ideal model and the abandoning of the Greek idea of a hierarchical and "objective" natural cosmos, to the emergence, in the second wave, of history as mediator between the is and the ought; from history, thus understood, to historicism strictly speaking appears but a short step; it is enough to conceive of historicity on the model of the "cunning of reason" (the idea that reason and the rational society are actualized not through reason itself, but through its other, by "passion," i.e., without man's consciously willing it). Strauss sees this in Kant's philosophy of history;[1] from Kant on, the distinction between good and evil, between the is and the ought, became blurred in favor of a secularization of the idea of providence that is the starting point of historicism: "In proportion as the providential order came to be regarded as intelligible to man, and therefore evil came to be regarded as evidently necessary or useful, the prohibition against doing evil lost its evidence. Hence various ways of action which were previously condemned as evil could now be regarded as good. The goals of human action were lowered. But it is precisely a lowering of these goals which modern political philosophy consciously intended from its very beginning" (*NR*, 317).

In his "Three Waves of Modernity" Strauss defines the first stage of this modern political philosophy: "[its] characteristics . . . were the reduction of the moral and political problem to a technical problem, and the concept of nature as in need of being overlaid by civilization as a mere artifact" ("TW," 84). This definition becomes clear when we refer it to what Strauss here sees[2] as the basic principle of Machiavelli's political ideas. The principle is twofold: the political question is first understood as based on the existence or nonexistence of the ought, and, correspondingly, the Greek notion of chance is, if not wholly, then at least partially thrown out: "[M]any have imagined commonwealths and principalities which never were, because they looked at how men ought to live instead of how men do in fact live. Machiavelli opposes to the idealism of traditional political philosophy a realist approach to political things. But this is only half of the truth (or in other words his realism is of a peculiar kind). The other half is stated by Machiavelli in these terms: fortuna is a woman who can be controlled by the use of force" ("TW," 84). We can see the close connection between these two statements when we see that their very conjunction suggests the destruction of classical philosophy: "[C]lassical political philosophy was a quest for the best political order, or the best regime as a regime most conducive to the practice of virtue or of how men should live, and . . . according to classical political philosophy the establishment of the best regime depends necessarily on uncontrollable elusive fortuna or chance" ("TW," 84). Machiavelli thus undertook to achieve mastery over fortune by lowering the standard by which the best regime is measured: "Machiavelli consciously lowers the standard of social action. His lowering of the standards is meant to lead to a higher probability of actualization of that scheme which is constructed in accordance with the lowered standards. Thus, the dependence on chance is reduced: chance will be conquered" ("PP," 41).[3]

This, I believe, shows the real meaning of the formula according to which, in the first wave of modernity, the political question is "reduced to a technical problem":[4] in the "lowering of the goal," which sanctions a "conquest of fortune," it is indeed the advent of technology that is at stake and this in the course of a twofold process: on the one hand, nature sinks from the rank of the hierarchical, meaningful cosmos of final causes and becomes pure chaos, neutral and devoid of meaning; on the other hand, human knowledge ceases to be "fundamentally receptive" ("TW," 87) and becomes activity directed toward the mastery of the disordered chaos that nature has become in the eyes of modern science:

> The rejection of final causes (and therewith also of the concept of chance) destroyed the theoretical basis of classical political philosophy. . . . [M]an calls nature before the tribunal of his reason; he "puts nature to the question"; knowing is a kind of making; human understanding prescribes nature its laws; man's power is infinitely greater than was hitherto believed; not only can man transform corrupt human matter into incorrupt human matter, or conquer chance—all truth and meaning originate in man; they are not inherent in a cosmic order which exists independently of man's activity. . . . Conquest of nature implies that nature is the enemy, a chaos to be reduced to order; everything good is due to man's labor rather than to nature's gift: nature supplies only the almost worthless materials. ("TW," 87, 88)

According to this analysis, which clearly echoes Heidegger on several points,[5] in modernity the "Greek relation" of man to nature is reversed, becoming a relation of mastery or domination, in short, a "technical" relation: while in classical thought nature "supplies . . . a standard wholly independent of man's will," one that limits that will,

thus leaving an opening for "the ineluctable power of chance" ("TW,"
85, 86), in modernity we see a complete reversal of this relation:
while in classical thought man is "by nature" "the measure of all
things," we might say that with the advent of modern science[6]—
"through freedom," actively—he becomes "the master and owner of
nature." In this sense—and here Strauss is reworking Heidegger—
"'Man is the measure of all things' is the very opposite of 'man is the
master of all things'" ("TW," 85).[7]

Strauss's thesis here reveals the connection between the reversal
of the very foundation of classical theories of natural right in the first
wave of modernity and the emergence, in the second wave, of a philosophy of history which—because it was rationalistic and deterministic, a philosophy of the necessity (the cunning of reason) of the
shift from the ideal to the real—opened the way to historicism and
the negation of political philosophy. Machiavelli's teachings imply a
complete reversal of the relation between morality and politics, a
reversal which Strauss seems to think was never undone in the second wave. We clearly need to understand this point to see how
Strauss saw that the "philosophies of freedom" representative of the
second wave of modernity, such as Kant's and Rousseau's, did not
contribute, despite appearances, to the renewal of political philosophy which they were intended to stimulate by a return to classical
philosophy. On this point Strauss's argument seems to be articulated
in three steps:

1. The lowering of the standard. The fact that the question of the
best regime is asked in relation to man (to passion), and not in relation to an "objective" or "substantial" natural order, implies a reversal
of the relation between morality and politics: while in classical philosophy politics is conceived of as concerning a preexisting ethical
order (a standard), from Machiavelli on, morality is not a condition
prior to reflection but, rather, an effect of politics:

> One must start from how men do live; one must lower one's sights.
> The immediate corollary is the reinterpretation of virtue: virtue must
> not be understood as that for the sake of which the commonwealth
> exists, but virtue exists exclusively for the sake of the common-
> wealth. . . . morality is not possible outside of political society; it pre-
> supposes political society; political society cannot be established and
> preserved by staying within the limits of morality, for the simple rea-
> son that the effect or the conditioned cannot precede the cause or
> condition. ("TW," 96).

So Strauss sees this reversal as an unavoidable result of the discarding of the "traditional approach" which was "based on the assumption that morality is something substantial: that it is a force in the soul of man, however ineffective it may be . . . in the affairs of states and kingdoms" ("PP," 41).

2. From then on, the way was potentially open for the emergence of a rationalistic and dialectical philosophy of history that saw the actualization of reason (of the true and of the good) effected by the opposite of reason: "Morality is possible only within a context which cannot be created by morality, for morality cannot create itself. The context within which morality is possible is created by immorality. Morality rests on immorality, justice rests on injustice, just as all legitimacy ultimately rests on revolutionary foundations" ("PP," 41–42).[8] And in connection with this, Strauss offers several formulas clearly indicating the link between the emergence of theories of the cunning of reason and this modern reversal[9] of the relation between the moral and the political, even citing the well-known passage from Kant's *Perpetual Peace* in which the philosopher affirms the possibility "for a nation of devils" to establish a just political society in which morality would become possible ("TW," 87).[10]

3. It is but a single step from the theory of the cunning of reason to historicism, for historicism already necessarily contains the idea that "the course of the world is the Tribunal of the world" and hence that the criterion of truth is success, so that to achieve a radical historicism, "it suffices" to deprive this theory of its systematic framework (see "TW," 23).

Thus we seem to have firmly established the connection between the first and the second waves, between the abandonment of the philosophical foundations of Greek thought and the slide into historicism. Yet how are we to understand—and this question is of course essential to our discussion, for on this point Fichte, even in his earliest political writings, explicitly cites the authority of Rousseau and Kant—the situation, in this "periodization" of political thought, of modern philosophies of the ought and the radical distinction between fact and rights? How are we to understand, for example, how we can include a thinker like Rousseau in a stream of thought that ends in the very negation of what seems to be the starting point of his thought? Doesn't Strauss himself recognize that Rousseau's philosophy begins with a reasoned critique of the first wave of modernity, in an attempt to get back to the classical view of natural right, insofar as Rousseau "protested in the name of virtue, of the genuine, nonutilitarian virtue of the classical republics against the degrading and enervating doctrines of his predecessors" ("TW," 89)?[11] How are we to understand the claim that "the return to pre-modern thought ... led, consciously or unconsciously, to a much more radical form of modernity" ("PP," 52)? How then are we to understand the claim that Rousseau, despite his reiterated distinction between fact and right, in reality led to a radical historicism, and hence that his "thought marks a decisive step in the secular movement which tries to guarantee the actualization of the ideal, or to prove the necessary coincidence of the rational and the real" ("PP," 53)?[12]

Here again, I shall merely indicate what I take to be the core of Strauss's argument: if, despite Rousseau's apparent return to a classical problematic, he in fact hastened the emergence of the modern view of historicity, it is because his attempt to restore the distinction between right and fact was made in the first wave of modernity from the prospect opened by Hobbes: "The concept of history, i.e., of the historical process as a single process in which man becomes human without intending it, is a consequence of Rousseau's radicalization of the Hobbesian concept of the state of nature" ("TW," 90).

Unlike "Machiavellian realism," Hobbes's idea of the state of nature indicates the need for a return to the idea of natural law while still acknowledging the basic requirements of this realism: "It was the difficulty implied in the substitution of merely political virtue for moral virtue or the difficulty implied in Machiavelli's admiration for the lupine policies of republican Rome that induced Hobbes to attempt the restoration of the moral principles of politics—i.e., of natural law—on the plane of Machiavelli's 'realism'" (NR, 179–80). Hence the ambiguity in the Hobbesian idea of the state of nature which seems to hark back to the classical tradition (with the search for a natural or moral "standard" with which to measure political requirements), but which radically transfigures it in other respects by subjecting it to the strictly modern requirement of realism; we find the solution to this ambiguity in the fact that the ideal of nature ceases to designate a goal or perfection but simply describes the original state of man:

> The predominant tradition had defined natural law with a view to the
> end or the perfection of man as a rational and social animal. What
> Hobbes attempted to do on the basis of Machiavelli's fundamental ob-

jection to the utopian teaching of the tradition, although in opposition to Machiavelli's own solution, was to maintain the idea of natural law but to divorce it from the idea of man's perfection; only if natural law can be deduced from how men actually live . . . can it be effectual or of practical value. The complete basis of natural law must be sought, not in the end of man, but in his beginning, in the *prima naturae* or, rather, in the *primum naturae*. What is most powerful in most men most of the time is not reason but passion . . . Natural law must be deduced from the most powerful of all passions (*NR*, 195).

As different from Hobbes's as it is, Rousseau's conception of the state of nature echoes Hobbes on one essential point: the break with the Greek idea of a natural teleology.[12] Furthermore, despite appearances, says Strauss, Rousseau arrived at his own conception of the state of nature by radicalizing Hobbes's principles; if we admit that man in the state of nature is solitary and therefore that his social nature is not innate, we must think of man in the state of nature as lacking everything that is produced through contact with others and hence as deprived of both vice and reason.[14] "From this we can understand best why Rousseau replaced the traditional definition of man as a rational animal by a new definition. Furthermore, since natural man is prerational, he is utterly incapable of any knowledge of the law of nature which is the law of reason. . . . Natural man is premoral in every respect: he has no heart. Natural man is subhuman" (*NR*, 270–71). Thus, according to Strauss, by rigorously applying Hobbes's own principles, Rousseau was led to deny natural man not merely sociability but also all forms of rationality.[15]

Strauss claims that this nonteleological conception of nature has a number of implications that gradually but inevitably brought forward the idea of history whose theorization was to be the doing of German idealism: the first and probably most important implication is Rousseau's repetition of the modern relation, already established by Machiavelli and Hobbes, between morality and politics. We have already glimpsed the form this reversal took in Machiavelli. In Hobbes, it reveals itself, as a result of his conception of the state of nature, in the design of the political sphere to satisfy individual rights (which the individual possesses through natural law) and not as establishing duties: "The state has the function, not of producing or promoting a virtuous life, but of safeguarding the natural right of each. . . . By transplanting natural law on the plane of Machiavelli, Hobbes certainly originated an entirely new type of political doctrine. The premodern natural law doctrine taught the duties of man;

41

if they paid any attention at all to his rights, they conceived of them as essentially derivative from his duties" (NR, 181–82).

In accordance with the demands of "Machiavellian realism," Hobbes's reversal of the moral/political relation characteristic of modernity in general thus takes the form of a reversal of the relation between rights and duties: the reason is that "the actualization of a social order that is defined in terms of man's duties is necessarily uncertain and even improbable. . . . Quite different is the case of a social order that is defined in terms of the rights of man. For the rights in question express, and are meant to express, something that everyone actually desires anyway" (NR, 182–83). Hence we see that, despite the return to the idea of a natural law, Hobbes remains thoroughly "modern," i.e., Machiavellian: "If the only unconditional moral fact is the natural right of each to his self-preservation, and therefore all obligations to others arise from contract, justice becomes identical with the habit of fulfilling one's contracts. Justice no longer consists in complying with standards that are independent of human will" (NR, 187).

So in subjecting the very idea of nature to the demands of consistent realism, Hobbes was merely extending the movement that, suppressing any idea of a natural or "objective" teleology, leads to the "reduction" of the moral act to its simply human dimension. And, according to Strauss, Rousseau inherited this modern conception of the relation between rights and duties by repeating Hobbes's idea of the state of nature as man's original state. This claim may seem paradoxical: haven't we admitted that, by deepening Hobbes's concept of the state of nature, Rousseau was somehow abandoning the "utilitarianism" of the thinkers of the first wave? Doesn't this abandonment therefore represent an unmistakable return to the duality of the is and the ought that is indispensable to a political philosophy? Strauss seems to recognize this when he emphasizes that Rousseau "was satisfied that happiness as Hobbes understood it is indistinguishable from constant misery and that Hobbes's and Locke's 'utilitarian' understanding of morality is inadequate: morality must have a more solid support than calculation" (NR, 280). Nevertheless, Strauss holds that, despite appearances, Rousseau was completely dependent on the new conception of the relations between law or rights and duty, between politics and morality, and if he remained a prisoner of this modern outlook, it was very much as a realistic thinker.

This needs to be explained if we are to understand how Strauss saw the modern and essentially realist philosophies of the ought as leading to historicism and the negation of political philosophy, so that modernity as a whole is prehistoricist. Indeed, if the ethical question is essentially one of "limitation," that of the distinction between "liberty and license,"[16] Strauss holds that in his theory of the general will Rousseau again resolved this question in a "realistic" way, for "his teaching ... can be regarded as the outcome of the attempt to find a 'realistic' substitute for the traditional natural law. According to that teaching, the limitation of human desires is affected not by the ineffectual requirements of man's perfection, but by the recognition in all others of the same right which one claims for one's self; all others necessarily take an effective interest in the recognition of their rights. . . . This being the case, my desire transforms itself into a rational desire by being 'generalized,' i.e., by being conceived as the content of a law which binds all members of society equally; a desire which survives the test of 'generalization' is, by this very fact, proved to be rational and hence just" (*NR*, 276–77).

Once again, it is difficult to see how, in this doubtful argument, Rousseau escapes the utilitarianism of the thinkers of the first wave. And the difficulty may be at the core of Strauss's critique of "philosophies of freedom." Note, however, that Strauss tries to find an answer to it by underscoring the ambiguity of Rousseau's attempt to break with the utilitarian conception of natural law while remaining faithful to the requirements of realism:

> In trying to restore an adequate understanding of happiness and of morality, he had recourse to a considerably modified version of traditional natural theology, but he felt that even that version of natural theology was exposed to 'insoluble objections.' To the extent to which he was impressed by the power of these objections, he was compelled to attempt to understand human life by starting from the Hobbesian notion of the primacy of right or of freedom as distinguished from the primacy of perfection or virtue or duty. He attempted to graft the notion of unconditional duties and of nonmercenary virtue onto the Hobbesian notion of the primacy of freedom or of right. He admitted, as it were, that duties must be conceived of as derivative from rights or that there is no natural law, properly speaking, which antedates the human will (*NR*, 280).

From this ambiguity in Rousseau's thought, we can now "deduce" Strauss's two main criticisms of it, i e., the fact that it leads to the modern concept of historicity and that the moral question about the distinction between liberty and license is resolved not by an "objective" standard external to the human will but by the idea of a mere generalization of self-interest; so that, if I understand Strauss's critique, Rousseau's modernity would consist less in suppressing the idea of the ought than in (1) presenting it as the product of a historical process and (2) emptying it of any "objective" content.

Let us look at these two closely connected points: if the radical abandonment of any teleological reference leads Rousseau to go even further than Hobbes in radically "desubstantializing" the idea of nature and hence denying natural man any quality other than perfectibility and the sentiment of pity, it follows that "human nature" reduces to what man acquires through his own efforts in the historical process: "Rousseau . . . saw that man in the state of nature is a man stripped of everything which he has acquired by his own efforts. Man in the state of nature is subhuman or prehuman; his humanity or rationality have been acquired in a long process. In post-Rousseauan language, man's humanity is due not to nature but to history, to the historical process" ("TW," 90).[17] Thus, the idea of nature is almost wholly replaced by that of history, the initial nature of man consisting, if I may say so, in his lacking a nature, in being simply indefinitely "perfectible": "Man is by nature good because he is by nature that subhuman being which is capable of becoming either good or bad. There is no natural constitution of man to speak of: everything specifically human is acquired. . . . There are no natural obstacles to man's almost unlimited progress or to his power of liberating himself from evil. For the same reason, there are no natural obstacles to man's almost unlimited degradation. . . . Man has no nature in the precise sense which would set a limit to what he can make out of himself" (*NR*, 271).

It is precisely at this point that we can finally spot what Strauss sees as the weakness of Rousseau's position, the ambiguity at the core of the idea of the ought: on the one hand, if the state of nature is "subhuman," it seems impossible to find in it any standard for measuring possible political requirements, and then we are ineluctably referred to history: "If the state of nature is subhuman, it is absurd to go back to the state of nature in order to find in it the norm for man. Hobbes had denied that man has a natural end. He had believed that he could find a natural or nonarbitrary basis of right in man's beginnings. Rousseau showed that man's beginnings lack all human traits. On the basis of Hobbes's premise, therefore,it became necessary to abandon altogether the attempt to find the basis of right in nature, in human nature." And therefore, if "man's humanity is the product of the historical process," it seems that the only "solution" is "to seek the standard of human action in the historical process" (*NR*, 274). Rousseau, however, who is still a philosopher, rejects this historicist solution because of its patent absurdity: "He realized that . . . the purpose [of the historical process] cannot be recognized except if there are trans-historical standards. The historical process cannot be recognized as progressive without previous knowledge of the end or purpose of the process. . . . It is, then, not knowledge of the historical process but knowledge of the true public right which supplies man with the true standard" (*NR*, 274).

So we see that Rousseau was not the originator of a historicism, for he preserved, in a sense that remains to be spelled out, the idea of the ought, of a standard transcending history. Strauss's critique thus concerns the nature of this standard as purely "formal," purely human, and in no way substantial or "objective." To understand this critique—which Strauss extended to all philosophies of freedom, which is to say the whole of German idealism—, we face the paradox that the state of nature, though designating a subhuman state, still serves as the standard, because Strauss saw the *Social Contract* as an attempt to define a political order that supplies the best approximation of the state of nature: "Civil society must therefore be transcended in the direction not of man's highest end but of his beginning, of his earliest past. Thus the state of nature tended to become for Rousseau a positive standard. . . . [T]he good life consists in the closest approximation to the state of nature which is possible on the level of humanity. On the political plane that closest approximation is achieved by a society which is constructed in conformity with the requirements of the social contract" (*NR*, 282).

So it must be admitted that the state of nature has two meanings, that it describes not just man's original condition but also a positive standard,[18] and that for this reason Rousseau still retains the idea of the ought and refuses to let it dissolve into "Machiavellian realism." Strauss's critique can then only concern the content of this "idea": if the subhuman state of nature seems not to yield any human norm, and, moreover, historical progress is devoid of meaning because of the lack of a transcendent standard for measuring this progress, how are we to think of the good and just political order as a return to our origins? What element in this state of undetermined and prehuman nature may serve as a positive criterion? Paradoxically, Strauss sees Rousseau using the criterion of this very indeterminacy, understood as "perfectibility" or freedom,[19] so that if Rousseau kept the importance of the notion of the state of nature, "the notion of the state of nature ... guaranteed the individual's radical independence.... In fact, [Rousseau] tends to identify freedom with virtue.... Above all, he suggests that the traditional definition of man be replaced by a new definition according to which not rationality but freedom is the specific distinction of man" (*NR,* 278–79). So that what seems to be the defect in Rousseau's state of nature, i.e., its being subhuman and hence indeterminate and unable to provide norms, was in reality "in Rousseau's eyes its perfect justification: the very indefiniteness of the state of nature as a goal of human aspiration made that state the ideal vehicle of freedom" (*NR,* 294).

It is on this precise point that Strauss sees the basic danger in Rousseau's thinking and in the philosophies of freedom that followed Rousseau's lead: adopting this fundamental indeterminacy as a standard means that the distinction between liberty and license tends to disappear, lacking all substantial reference: "To have a reservation against society in the name of the state of nature means to have a reservation against society without being either compelled or able to indicate the way of life or the cause or the pursuit for the sake of which that reservation is made. The notion of a return to the state of nature on the level of humanity was the ideal basis for claiming a freedom from society which is not a freedom for something. It was the ideal basis for an appeal from society to something indefinite and indefinable" (*NR,* 294). In short, what Strauss denounces as thoroughly dangerous in Rousseau's thought is the modern idea of freedom understood as the absence of "human nature" or, to repeat Fichte's formula, of being "initially nothing," unlike an animal which is, if only by instinct, always something definite;[20] Strauss contrasts this freedom with what is "justified by reference to something higher than the individual or than man as mere man" and which alone "establishes a tenable distinction between freedom and license" (*NR,* 294).

In accordance with this distinction between the two types of freedom and, it seems to me, to keep its significance (only the Greek view of freedom which refers to an "objective," nonhuman limitation, allows us to distinguish liberty from license), Strauss is obliged to interpret Rousseau's view of the general will and its echo in Kant's *Critique of Practical Reason* in terms of self-interest: this debatable interpretation is really the only one that allows us to maintain the priority of classical freedom (an "objective" limitation by virtue) over modern freedom (perfectibility, hence indeterminacy) by exposing the arbitrary character of modern freedom: thus Strauss doesn't hesitate to write that "if the ultimate criterion of justice becomes the general will, i.e., the will of a free society, cannibalism is as just as its opposite. Every institution hallowed by a folk-mind has to be regarded as sacred" ("PP," 53). This thesis, which makes Rousseau into a strictly realist thinker, rests on the idea that in the modern view the limitation on freedom can come only from other freedoms; then we see how Rousseau prefigures, for Strauss, the essential work of German idealism: the rationalist philosophy of history:

> Rousseau's thought makes a decisive step in the secular movement which tries to guarantee the actualization of the ideal, or to prove the necessary coincidence of the rational and the real, or to get rid of that which essentially transcends every possible human reality. The assumption of such a transcendence had permitted earlier men to make a tenable distinction between liberty and license. License consists in doing what one lists; liberty consists in doing in the right manner the good only; and our knowledge of the good must come from a higher principle, from above. These men acknowledged a limitation of license which comes from above, a vertical limitation. On the basis of Rousseau, the limitation of license is effected horizontally by the license of other men. I am just if I grant to every other man the same right which I claim for myself, regardless of what these rights may be. The horizontal limitation is preferred to the vertical limitation because it seems to be more realistic: the horizontal limitation, the limitation of my claim by the claims of others, is self-enforcing ("PP," 53).

This means that if the limitation on freedom is the result of a ratio of forces between possibly illegitimate requirements, the outcome (the "resultant") of this conflict may also be radically illegitimate in the face of the requirement of vertical limitation, even when it accords (which it does by definition at some moment in the historical process) with the requirements of a horizontal limitation: let the general will opt for cannibalism and, according to Strauss, there is nothing in Rousseau's political thought to prevent this, for such behavior could only be limited vertically, in accordance with an "objective" order.

This criticism of Rousseau helps us see Strauss's two main objections to the political thought that he believed common to German idealism:

1. First, this interpretation suggests that Rousseau's philosophy points toward a rationalist theory of history, a theory of the "cunning of reason" showing the necessary coincidence of the real and the rational, the is and the ought: "The German philosophers who took up his problem thought that a reconciliation is possible, and that rec-

onciliation can be brought about, or has already been brought about, by History. . . . Philosophy of history shows the essential necessity of the actualization of the right order. There is no chance in the decisive respect, i.e., the same realistic tendency which led to the lowering of the standards in the first wave led to philosophy of history in the second wave" ("PP," 55–56). Aiming to do away with the distinction between the real and the ideal, Rousseau's German successors thus interpreted his philosophy correctly and supplemented it with a philosophy of history that is no doubt important, but in no way decisive.

2. The second objection to German idealism more directly concerns the "horizontal" workings of the limitation of freedoms: we have seen how deficient the classical view (the "vertical limitation") would find the result of this limitation, because in the modernity launched by Rousseau, "it is then the mere generality of a will which vouches for its goodness" without its being "necessary to have recourse . . . to any consideration of what man's nature, his natural perfection, requires" ("TW," 92).

Now Strauss saw the simple radicalization of this view as supplying the underpinnings of the practical philosophy of German idealism, i.e., of Kantian morality: Rousseau's conception

> reached full clarity in Kant's moral doctrine: the sufficient test for the goodness of maxims is their susceptibility of becoming principles of universal legislation; the mere form of rationality, i.e., universality, vouches for the goodness of the content. Therefore, the moral laws, as laws of freedom, are no longer understood as natural laws. Moral and political ideals are established without reference to man's nature: man is radically liberated from the tutelage of nature. Arguments against the ideal which are taken from man's nature, as known by the uncontestable experience of the ages, are no longer of importance. . . . [T]he only guidance regarding the future, regarding what men ought to do or aspire to, is supplied by reason. Reason replaces nature. This is the meaning of the assertion that the ought has no basis whatever in the is ("TW," 92).

2. The Return to Classical Thought

In the next chapter I shall come back to the hidden difficulties in what I take to be this unacceptable reading of the philosophies of the second wave. For the moment I shall merely note that for Strauss there clearly follows the necessity of making a return—against the whole of modernity which separates us as surely as a "screen" ("PP,"

24)—to the "Golden Age" of political philosophy, to that "purest expression of nonhistoricist thought" represented by Greek philosophy. Classical philosophy does appear to contrast with modernity on four points, which define the preconditions for genuine political reflection:

1. Being philosophical, classical political thought is first the discovery,[20] against authority, of the idea of nature understood as "standard," and it thereby initiates reflection about man's ability to transcend the given: "The emergence of philosophy radically affects man's attitude toward political things. . . . Originally, the authority par excellence or the root of all authority was the ancestral. Through the discovery of nature, the claim of the ancestral is uprooted; philosophy appeals from the ancestral to the good, to that which is good intrinsically, to that which is good by nature. . . . By uprooting the authority of the ancestral, philosophy recognizes that nature is *the* authority. It would be less misleading, however, to say that, by uprooting authority, philosophy recognizes nature as *the* standard" (*NR*, 91–92). So the discovery of the idea of nature thus appears as the first and "necessary condition for the emergence of the idea of natural right" (*NR*, 93) and therefore also of political philosophy since "philosophy as distinguished from myth came into being when nature was discovered" (*NR*, 82).

2. This idea is the basis of the notion of the ought without which the very idea of natural right would obviously make no sense. Again, we need to make clear that in classical thought the ought has a strictly natural and teleological meaning that plainly distinguishes it from the modern view of freedom: "Natural right in its classic form is connected with a teleological view of the universe. All natural beings have a natural end, a natural destiny, which determines what kind of operation is good for them" (*NR*, 7), so that 'we must . . . distinguish between those human desires and inclinations which are natural and those which originate in conventions. Furthermore, we must distinguish between those human desires and inclinations which are in accordance with human nature and therefore good for man, and those which are destructive of his nature or his humanity and therefore bad. We are thus led to the notion of a life, a human life, that is good because it is in accordance with nature" (*NR*, 94–95). Thus there is enough distance between nature and the real to establish the idea of the ought, but this distance is sufficiently reduced for these two terms not to be so radically cut off from each other that their coincidence would prove impossible: in short, we are still far from

"this modern view" which, "rejecting nature as the standard," holds that "Nature and Freedom, Reality and Norm, the Is and the Ought, appeared to be wholly independent of one another" (*NR*, 96).[22]

3. The question of the very being of the social consequently emerges in the vaster, properly philosophical inquiry into the essence of the natural order: in this sense, the political is not directly thought of as a human construction, like a product of some action, still less as the manifestation of some absolute rationality since for that matter the "natural is here understood in contrast to what is human, too human" ("PP," 24).[23] It is within a larger teleological order that "the best regime" becomes the guiding theme of political philosophy,[24] i.e., the object of a questioning in which man's relation to the natural cosmos is shot through with mystery; for the core of classical political philosophy is more the search for a cosmology than for the solution to a cosmological problem,[25] the sole prerogative of man— but this prerogative may be essential—being questioning; it comes from the fact that "the human soul is the only part of the whole which is open to the whole";[26] but as long as this interrogation is philosophically rigorous and refuses to yield to what might justly be called "ideology," it never denies the mystery inhering in the very core of man's relation to the truth about everything.[27]

4. The permanence of this "mystery"—which is translated in Socrates as the fact that knowledge cannot claim to be anything other than a "knowledge of ignorance"—explains the absence, assuredly essential for Strauss, of "a philosophy of history" in classical political philosophy,[28] i.e., the absence of a rationalization of the historical process by which the "best regime" would be conceived as the right one to be actualized necessarily. On the contrary, its actualization depends in the final analysis on "fortune," for example, in Plato, on the coincidence between political power and philosophy,[29] so that because man here is quite unable to posit himself as "master and owner of nature," "the political problem" does not in any way shrink to a "technical problem" ("TW," 87).

Thus in possession—at least as a guiding thread for philosophical inquiry—of a natural standard that is both transcendental and "objective," the deeply nonhumanist classical political philosophy appears located at the opposite poles from the two resolutely modern figures negating political philosophy: historicism and positivism. The political writings of German idealism—reduced, in its seemingly least "realistic" figure, the *Critique of Practical Reason*, to merely a huge attempt to justify and sanctify reality—thus would in essence merely consist in (1) producing a philosophy of history that tends to give a systematic "proof" of the necessary coincidence of the real and the ideal, and (2) generalizing the indeterminate and formal concept of a reciprocal limitation of freedoms, thus definitively sanctifying the liquidation of any ethical standard against which politics could be measured. Thus, from German idealism to the ultimate historicist and positivist negations of political philosophy, there would indeed be only a step, so that in this second wave of modernity the search for a plurality of ideas of historicity, even the renewal of an authentically philosophical political inquiry, would be roundly condemned.

At this point, however, I would like to voice the suspicion that Strauss's proposed periodization of the history of political philosophy—a periodization whose orientation is easily seen by his concern to decide the quarrel between the ancients and the moderns in favor of the former—actually glosses over the tensions and diversity that manifested themselves in the course of the second wave—tensions that it is far from certain were harmoniously reconciled by the "Hegelian coronation"—, and hence that Strauss's philosophy remains captive to a traditional univocal and linear view of the history of philosophy.

Without venturing a comprehensive critique of this periodization and its implied choice of a "classical," "objective," or "substantial" conception of morality, I shall try to indicate the reasons that should lead to questioning the image it tends to convey of German idealism.

C H A P T E R   T W O

The Limits of Strauss's Critique of Modernity: German Idealism and the Plurality of Modern Philosophies of History

1. A Reductive Reading of Rousseau and Kant

Strauss's reading of the "second wave" philosophies runs into two problems, one de jure and the other de facto. First, his criticism of the philosophies of freedom (implicit in his interpretation of Rousseau) contains some ambiguities, for the alleged "realism" supposed to prevail in a continuous way from Hobbes to Rousseau is not obvious. Second, not all the German philosophers of the period defined history as the unconscious (unintended) and necessary actualization of man's humanity (and the reasonable and just order), for it was just this philosophy of history that the young Fichte[1] (inspired, moreover, by Kant's *Critique of Practical Reason*) meant radically to condemn. Strauss's claim that this idea of history is representative of German idealism thus paradoxically amounts to legitimizing Hegel's interpretation of the history of philosophy at the expense of the whole of Kant's and Fichte's practical philosophy[2]—paradoxically, not only because the analogy between Hegel's and Strauss's "fatalistic" and linear readings[3] is at least debatable, but also because this practical philosophy rightly represents the only attempt by a German idealist to restore rigorously—or rather, establish—the gulf between the is and the ought, and this—by disregarding their analysis as though one and the same movement was accomplished from Kant to Hegel—is precisely to forget that Hegel's philosophy was progressively formed through a critique of the ethical views of Kant (in the *Critique of Practical Reason* of course, but not only) and of Fichte,[4] as it is to forget that the Kant's and Fichte's practical philosophies also were formed in a polemic against "dogmatism" and, particularly for Fichte, deterministic theories of history.

Let us take up these two points and look at the ambiguities of Strauss's reading of Rousseau, particularly his claim to reduce the *So-*

cial Contract to a form of "realism" or utilitarianism: if, as Strauss believed, we should consider the society described in the *Social Contract* an "approximate return" to the state of nature, or as "the best approximation possible" to the life of natural man, how are we to see[5] as the lone goal of this society the fact of actualizing a "structure conducive to its self-preservation" and favoring freedom in the sense of simple "natural freedom"? In this view, the *Social Contract* is not a return to the state of nature but rather a remedy for its deterioration into a "state of barbarism" and eventually a Hobbesian state of nature. How then do we support the claim that the state of nature "tended for Rousseau to become a positive standard"?

It seems to me that the "logic" of Strauss's interpretation—even independent of the (no doubt) naive question of its "veracity"— should lead us to choose one or the other (but not both!) of the following alternatives. *Either* we make Rousseau a "realist" who firmly roots the ought in the is, and thus introduces the theme of the "cunning of reason": we will then privilege the theory of the general will, for the idea that it cannot err implies the necessity of the ought's coinciding with the is: we shall also interpret the social contract not as an approximation of the state of nature but only—which is different—as a remedy for its deterioration and hence a remedy for the historical state that Hobbes called the "state of nature" but that Rousseau deemed merely a relatively late era in history; from this viewpoint, we see that Rousseau's thought reduces to a mere "logical" consequence of Hobbes's philosophy. *Or,* on the contrary, we insist that Rousseau is not a "utilitarian," that he maintained a dual definition of the state of nature—as origin and also as a legal state of man—, that he meant to base morality on freedom and not on self-interest, and hence to deny the premises of historicism.[6] If this is so, however, aren't we also forced to admit (1) that Rousseau is not fully a realist (because, whatever particular form it takes, realism must anchor the necessity of actualizing the best regime in self-interest); (2) that, consequently, he maintains the difference between the is and the ought; and (3) that the social contract is not just a cure for the war of all against all but an attempt to bring about freedom (not just natural freedom but also "perfectibility"), the social contract then defining not the society most likely to ensure human happiness but the one consonant with "human nature," i.e., freedom? In other words, mustn't we admit that Rousseau's use of Hobbes's premises to transcend the Hobbesian state of nature puts him on a different plane from Hobbes, in that discovering the ideal of freedom in the state of nature, Rousseau discovers something that cannot be reduced to empirical self-interest and thus be called a "realism"?

The main problem with Strauss's interpretation thus seems to be its allowance of both these readings without the resulting manifest contradiction that seems to need thematizing, so that we are unsure whether Strauss's main criticism of Rousseau is that he accelerated the "realistic" movement toward historicism, or that he abandoned any reference to an objective and substantial ought in favor of one based in and through human freedom. Now, we easily see that these two criticisms, both present in Strauss's writings, are in fact incompatible: to base the ought on human freedom is to eschew any form of realism (Kant and Fichte make this idea quite clear in the well-known and profoundly anti-Hegelian thesis that the ideal is forever unattainable) and, conversely, to base the actualization of the ideal in self-interest is clearly to give up thinking of freedom in the way Rousseau, Kant, and Fichte did.[7] This is, moreover, the reason for which these philosophies of freedom, far from being stages along the way to Hegelianism, have on the contrary represented from the start—and Hegel is not mistaken about this—his most feared opponents. So it appears to me impossible to accept Strauss's hypothesis of "realism" in the philosophies of freedom (a realism that he attributes if not to Fichte, about whom he says little, at least to Rousseau and Kant), for—as Strauss himself shows, moreover—realism makes sense only if it entails some form of "utilitarianism."[8]

Thus, Strauss's only genuine objection to the modern philosophers of freedom—one he extends to Kant and Rousseau, but would no doubt find equally valid for Fichte—is directed, much more than at political realism, at the abandonment of reference to an "objective" and transcendent order or (which comes to the same thing) the modern idea of the limitation of freedom by the notion of universality. Thus we see how these "second wave" thinkers may be Strauss's most formidable opponents, for they uphold the difference between the is and the ought, and even the transcendence of the ought in relation to man: how could it be otherwise given the assertion that the perfect actualization of the ideal is impossible? And isn't it exactly this assertion that makes Kant's and Fichte's philosophies, for the same reason as Judaism, the premier examples for Hegel of the "unhappy consciousness"? Isn't it again the assertion of this transcendence that—as Max Horkheimer recalled,[9] noting the profound affinity between Judaism and critical philosophy—at least partially explains the considerable influence of Kantianism on German-Jewish thought?[10]

So the real difference between the modern philosophies of freedom and classical thought lies not, as Strauss suggests, in the modern philosophers' denial of the transcendence of the ideal but rather in their definition of the ideal as compatible with an authentic idea of man's humanity (freedom). So Strauss's own criteria permit these philosophies of freedom—if they ascribe some ethical significance to the transcendence of the ideal—to have all the features on which to base political ideas that are both nonhistoricist and nonpositivist.

Therefore, it appears that Strauss denies the underlying postulate of these philosophies of freedom more as a matter of a personal ethical choice than in the name of a genuine discussion of their principles. This is suggested by even a cursory analysis of Strauss's attack on the modern idea of universality as an ethical criterion: indeed, the assertion that "if the ultimate criterion of justice becomes the general will, ... cannibalism is as just as its opposite"—beyond its involving Strauss's manifest and indeed constant confusion of the general will with the majority will[11]—implies so obvious an absurdity that we can hardly take it as anything other than a piece of sophistry intended more to discredit an opponent than to refute him. Nevertheless, the stakes of this critique must have seemed crucial to Strauss, for he must have been aware of the "alternative" offered by the modern philosophies of the ought to the prospect of restoring classical thought, and of the objections that a "modern" view would raise against his plan.

So we should take a closer look at what Strauss's criticism may be leaving intact in this modernity whose meaning and scope it claims to have broadly forestalled. For though Strauss's criticisms of Rousseau's or Kant's concept of universality are clearly off target, it may also be that he missed the full ethical and political significance of their ideas: denying that the universality of a maxim is "sufficient" to guarantee its ethical character may indeed be to miss the conception of humanity, the theory of communication, and the criticism of ideology that this thesis contains in nucleo [12] for if the "horizontal limitation" is preferable to the heteronomy of determination by some naturality, it is in no way through a concern for "realism," as Strauss has it, but because if man is free and hence possesses, as distinct from things, neither "nature" nor "perfection,"[13] we must necessarily think of politics as a public space or common area of intersubjectivity, the essential property of the illusion or ideology being precisely to "objectivize" or reify man by reducing him to a mere exemplar of an objective concept. In short, what Strauss omits from his account of modernity is precisely its undeclared attempt to use the concept of "practical reason" to establish the ideal of freedom as the ought: in attacking the modern philosophy of history as a philosophy of "necessity," Strauss failed to specify that this necessity, if simply practical or ethical, in no way implies, as would a theoretical necessity, that the ideal is reducible to the real. In parallel, modernity's thesis that "political theory becomes the understanding of what has fostered practice, the understanding of the actual, and ceases to be the search for what had to be" merely confirms again, and actually repeats almost word for word, the Hegelian judgment that proclaims the triumph of intelligence over the will,[14] the victory of the theoretical view over the ethical view "still" characteristic of the doctrines of Kant and Fichte.

It is obviously difficult to determine exactly how far Strauss's masking of the ethical viewpoint in modernity is deliberate, i.e., in accordance with the "art of writing" of a philosopher who is addressing only "intelligent readers"[15] assumed to be capable of seeing something more than a simple blunder in an "unorthodox" reading: difficult indeed, since in this case the linear view of a history of philosophy going from one problem to another[16] is indeed perfectly orthodox, particularly when applied to German idealism in order to see in it just a "logical" development ineluctably dominated in the final instance by Hegelianism.[17]

Be that as it may, this view must be put in doubt, not only for reasons concerning its questionable textual accuracy—it does not stand up against a careful analysis of thinkers who, like Kant and Fichte, are assumed merely to represent a "stage"—but also because it contradicts Strauss's own argument against historicism and relativism; clearly, this project restores the ideal of the ought as a prerequisite for a critique of the positivity of the real. It was from this viewpoint that Strauss insisted on the necessity for man, faced with events like those in Germany during the 1930s, to assume his "responsibility" and to "answer the question of the good society" without evading it "by deferring to History or to any other power different from his own reason."[18] Now I confess to not seeing how a similar critique of historicism—and it would be easy, by rereading, for example, the introduction of *Natural Right and History,* to produce a number of quotations clearly showing the ethical necessity of nonsubmission to the positivity of the real—could dispense with reference to the modern notion of freedom as will or practical reason. What's more, how could the very idea of a distinctively human responsibility as the really critical unique power (since "any power" other than human reason is explicitly eschewed) be based on an absolute rejection of "modern humanism"? How also do we not see that, conversely, an "ought" thought of in purely "objectivist" or "substantialist" terms cannot remain an ought and still keep its critical power?

Let me be more specific. If the actualization of the ideal depends on fortune, and fortune is beyond man's control, shouldn't we irrevocably forgo all action meant to actualize the ideal, hence all critical activity? As Fichte shows, the philosophies of chance and of necessity are exactly equivalent from the viewpoint of a freedom that professes to be critical of the real;[19] if the actualization of the best regime depends on chance or necessity, what is the use of criticizing the real in the name of the ideal? In other words, doesn't any denunciation of the real in the name of the ideal—hence any rejection of historicism and relativism—presuppose, if only partially, the will to "conquer chance," to have some effect on reality? Doesn't it therefore imply some minimal concession to the modern ethical idea of freedom?

All of Strauss's argumentation here seems to me biased by the systematic concern to impose on the reader an alternative that eliminates these questions: either I admit the existence of a nonhuman, substantial, and "objective" ethical order, and thus support the difference between the is and the ought while also indicating a line clearly demarcating liberty from license; or—and this would be the drift of modern humanism—I give up this disparity and anchor the ideal in the real by means of a "realism" showing the necessity of reconciling the two terms in an idea of freedom that allows for no distinction between liberty and license. In short, Strauss's alternative is between nature and history, the choice in favor of history implying a strictly theoretical (not ethical) conception of the relations between the ideal and the real. I submit that this alternative masks a third possibility which is precisely the one envisaged by the philosophies of freedom. It is certainly permissible to cast doubt on Kant's or Fichte's ethical philosophy, which conceives of freedom as will or practical reason; but we do real violence to their ideas if we reduce them univocally to a stage in the process of submission to history. Furthermore, we cannot consistently eliminate the notions they pose themselves; when Kant's and Fichte's practical philosophies (like Strauss's criticism of Heidegger) see the actualization of the best regime as depending on chance, this is just as "historicist" as its depending on a theoretical necessity, for dependence on chance also puts the ideal outside the range of human intervention and so robs it of any critical power. From the viewpoint of ethical freedom, nature and history blend together much more than they are opposed, and Fichte's criticism of theories of the cunning of reason shows this by condemning all modern philosophies of necessity as thoroughly naturalistic.[20]

Conversely, if there is no classical "philosophy of history," as Strauss claims, there is at least an "idea" of history which, as we have seen, attributed the actualizability of the best regime to chance (therefore negating the principle of sufficient reason which sees classical thought as the absolute antithesis of modern realism); Fichte argues that this foreclosure of temporality inevitably implies the negation of any critical project concerning the positivity of the real, for exactly the same reason as the most rationalistic theory of the cunning of reason.

This difficulty—the fact that Strauss's implicit idea of history may be radically unsuitable for attacking historicism[21]—shows up more clearly when we see how Strauss condemns the modern view of the ought not just because of its "realist" aspect (because it supposedly produces confusion of the real with the ideal) but also because, with the abandonment of the classical idea of nature, the ought paradoxically proves completely separate from this is.[22] This criticism has been repeated by Pierre Manent,[23] who argues that the two viewpoints of modern philosophy, "the 'scientific' or 'realist' viewpoint—the sacralization of the 'fact'—and the 'moral' or 'utopian' viewpoint—the sacralization of 'rights'—are in reality accomplices." After showing how Machiavellian "realism" in fact implies "a transformation of the world no less radical than that ascribed to utopianism," Manent argues that Rousseau's distinction between fact and right is actually "just as complete a surrender to given realities as the one ascribed to Machiavellianism" which is disguised. On this final point, we see that this thesis fully accords with Strauss's thesis: Rousseau seems to restore classical thought by denouncing the utilitarianism of his predecessors, but he is in fact leading us to a "surrender to given realities" that prefigures historicism. Finally, as in Strauss, it is Hegelianism that triumphantly reconciles the two streams, and apparently without reminder or resistance: from this viewpoint, the philosophies that are "integrated" or "reconciled" in the supreme synthesis get only their just deserts, for their opposition involves a hidden complicity such that their mutual antagonism is, basically,

merely asking to be suppressed: "Machiavelli, Hobbes, and Hegel—
this is the progression of modern political thought in the guise of
realism or the sacralization of the fact; Rousseau, Kant, and again Hegel—this is the progression of modern thought in the guise of utopianism or the sacralization of rights. Hegel is the common term of
the two sequences. We know that he considered his system the cul-
mination of philosophy; at the very least, he completed modern philosophy by producing and revealing the unity of his apparently twofold and contradictory project."[24]

In this harmonious tripartite vision, where Fichte shines by his
absence, the violence of Hegel's reconciliation is both echoed and
legitimized, everything happening as though, since the tensions
piercing German idealism are merely apparent, the Hegelian dialectic was "at least true for modernity."[25] Furthermore, the way Manent
condemns the complicity between the tradition of right and that of
fact, still following Strauss in this, can only round back on its author:
for here Rousseau is attempting to base the "social imperative" on a
principle so far from the real that the ideal has no critical bearing:
"[T]o base the legitimacy of a society (human relationships) on the
autonomy of the individual is to base it on the most asocial principle
there is. . . . Therefore, the principle, the social imperative, cannot
enter into the reality of the society, into the social indicative. There
is an irreducible gap and incommunicability between the spheres of
legitimacy and of reality. . . . so basing the just society purely on
rights tends to leave fact as it is."[26]

This objection, which reflects an ambiguity in Strauss's interpretation (does Rousseau help bring together the is and the ought
through the mediation of history, or does he separate them so that
they are totally unconnected?), also points up the two main difficulties in it: if in Rousseau the "complicity with fact" is the result of the
ideal's unactualizability or lack of connection with the real (but,
again, how then is he a "realist"?), should we not a fortiori level the
same accusation against classical thought? How could the ideal be
more widely and more certainly distant from the real than by the
notion of chance? If the actualization of the best regime depends on
chance, isn't this regime radically and definitively cut off from fact? If
the philosopher can never "bring about" the "happy coincidence" for
which he "can only wish or pray" (*NR*, 199–200), what even minimal
sense can some critical intervention have, even if limited to the mere
publication of a book attacking historicism? It is plainly impossible
to keep the ideal and the real connected if the "mediation" is left to

chance, and then we have little idea what would stand up to Manent's argument against classical philosophy (particularly Plato's) as described by Strauss.[27] This internal difficulty in Strauss's project must be connected to the more general question about the possibility of a critique of historicism based uniquely on the classical concept of nature.[28]

But a second, extrinsic difficulty adds to the first one: for Rousseau is in fact not at all representative of what Manent calls the "moral and utopian viewpoint." I will offer only two points of evidence here: first, we note that Manent's criticism repeats almost word for word (no doubt inadvertently) what Fichte says about Rousseau in his "Lectures on the Vocation of the Scholar."[29] So it is somewhat surprising to hear Rousseau called a representative of the "philosophers of freedom," for Manent's criticism of "utopia" does not apply to Kant (whose philosophy of history is, strictly speaking, no more a theoretical realism than a moral utopianism) or to Fichte (who criticized Rousseau for too sharply separating fact and right). In another connection, it is enough to look at Fichte's philosophy of rights to see—something already well demonstrated by Georges Gurvitch[30]—that it is not at all a legal individualism (and Kant's *Science of Right* makes the same point): it is just in the cardinal distinction between rights and ethics that Fichte's and Kant's political ideas explicitly diverge from Rousseau's;[31] so that making Kant's or Fichte's critique depend on Rousseau's—and thereby assenting to Hegel's judgment about all his "predecessors"—is doubly arbitrary. It fails to take account—which would be interesting to resolve the question of the relations between fact and right—of the specifics of the philosophy of history and of the philosophy of rights for each of the writers in question.

It therefore seems to me—and this I see as the central difficulty in Strauss's thought—that a serious attack on historicism and positivism must include some thoughts about historicity—thinking as mediation between the real and the ideal—and cannot take refuge in a supposedly "naturalist" and ahistorical position. Far from remaining aloof from all philosophy of history, Strauss's philosophy suggests a classical conception of historicity as "chance," such that what is at stake here in the opposition between nature (in the classical sense), history (in Strauss's sense), and freedom (in Kant's and Fichte's sense) is the conflict between three ideas of historicity:[32]

- The idea that the temporal process is not conceived on the basis of "subjectivity" (from the human subject's logical or ethical principles) and hence does not depend on the principle of sufficient reason or man's free intentional activity; consigned to "otherness," the historical process thus appears largely dominated by "chance" or "destiny." This is basically the classical conception of historicity "restored" by Heidegger (and Strauss) in the name of "the history of Being."

- The modern realist idea that the mediation between the real and the ideal occurs through a deterministic causal process that is both necessary and ineluctable because it is wholly governed by the principle of sufficient reason. This view of historicity, which Strauss sees stemming from Machiavelli, culminates in the Hegelian theory of the cunning of reason.

- The modern nonrealist conception that thinks of the relations between the real and the ideal in the ethical terms of freedom and the ought, and that culminates in Fichte.

I do not propose here to analyze how these three ideas of historicity may be articulated. What has been said up to this point should convince us of the need to question the idea of a univocality—if not in appearance, then at least fundamentally—of the "philosophies of freedom" constitutive of German idealism. This task presupposes that I first indicate what is meant here by "German idealism"[33] and that we determine what its philosophical project and shared political aim was; for it is from a certain communality of project that we will be able to see the irreducibility of the divergences.

2. German Idealism and the Different Approaches to the System

Without claiming here to exhaust the meaning and scope of German idealism, I think we can define the philosophical project that seems to be common to these idealists as a "project of a system." All the evidence suggests that post-Kantian thinking about the *Critique of Pure Reason* has two general purposes: on the one hand, to get rid of "the thing in itself," and, correspondingly, to give a genuinely deductive form to what in Kant was deductive in name only.[34] Thus, the goal of German idealism was the creation of a system, which then becomes the "rallying cry and most deep-seated requirement."[35] German idealism then appears as the stage when the philosophical project was to produce a system, in the sense of putting into order everything that is for a reason able to produce the intelligibility of

everything real, to conceptualize every field of reality, to determine
the logic of the relations between the various fields, and therefore to
situate some fields in relation to others in a complete totality where
the positioning of each element makes sense only in reference to the
logical structure of the whole—a structure from which the assign-
ment of each element to its place and function is rationally deduced.
The philosophical orientation of German idealism is thus defined as
participation in a project of rational systematicity in which the unifying principle of the multiple is rationality (subjectivity) or the power
to produce and link up concepts.

In spelling out the meaning of this project—which will help us
see how philosophical and political ideas are articulated in German
idealism—, we need to keep in mind that the term "system" is used
in two senses, one methodical, the other ontological:[36]

- Methodically, the notion of system simply designates the mode
  of presentation or exposition of philosophy: philosophers from
  Kant to Hegel never ceased repeating that what is best suited for
  philosophical exposition is the system, for the system is precisely "what first raises ordinary knowledge to the rank of science," so that "an unsystematic philosophy is unscientific."[37] In
  this sense, the system, in contrast to the "aggregate," is defined
  as "the unity of manifold modes of knowledge in one idea," i.e.,
  as a genuine organic unity: "The whole is thus an organized
  unity (*articulatio*) and not an aggregate (*coacervatio*); it may
  grow from within (*per intussusceptionem*), but not by external
  addition (*per oppositionem*). It is thus like an animal body . . ."[38]
  Thus the essence of the system is said to be a philosophical
  method: it unites the multiplicity of pieces of knowledge in a
  totality of elements whose cohesion, interdependence, and in-
  tegration are modeled on a living organism.
- This reference to the living creature helps us understand the
  second, ontological meaning of the idea of a system, revealing
  the analogy between an apparently formal philosophical
  method and an element arising from reality. As Alain Renaut remarks, "This discovery of the system as a mode of being of a
  type of being is decisive: it helps us understand the system as
  the mode in which not only a type of (organic) being exists, but
  indeed the totality of being":[39] the transition—by which what
  seemed simply formal and methodical comes to characterize the
  very structure of reality, if we think of the totality of the real as,

so to speak, an organized being—presupposes a certain "ontology" or definition of what is the essence of the real or, if you will, the "reality of the real." This ontology is easy to identify; it involves the Hegelian formula that "the real is rational" and the "rational, real": for when what is basically a mere subjective form of rationality (because the required systematic deduction of the multiple from the one is, as Heidegger reminds us,[40] itself merely a formal prerequisite of the mathematical proof) is taken for the very structure of the real, this obviously is done on the basis of an ontology in which the real is defined a priori as consistent with the principles of a logical and mathematical rationality.[41]

Having defined the notion of system, we still need to note that its relation to German idealism rests first of all on a "historical" argument: in all probability, the term "system" first appeared in the title of a philosophical work, Leibniz's *New System of Nature and of the Communication of Substances* of 1695. So we must see if not the historical reasons for the appearance of this new usage—where Leibniz's predecessors more readily used "discourse" or "meditations"—at least its philosophical preconditions.

In his book on Schelling, Heidegger tries to answer this question by indicating the six "main conditions for the first construction of a system (*ST*, 30) His analysis highlights the primacy of mathematics in the constitution of the philosophical idea of the system: the mathematical—in that it "is a definitely oriented interpretation of the nature of knowledge in general," an interpretation according to which there belongs to knowledge the self-originating foundation of what is knowable in terms of and within first principles which need no foundation"(*ST*, 30)—is, as it were, triply appropriate to the philosophical project of a system: first, the requirement that theorems be deduced from a minimal number of first principles (the principle of economy) already tends to bring about an articulation of the one of the multiple required for the constitution of a system. Next, the requirement that first principles be certain or self-evident "means to *search* within the total realm of beings for the something knowable which in itself admits of a corresponding foundation of itself. . . . Knowledge considers itself founded when it is certain of itself" (*ST*, 30). The mathematical certainty that is supposed to characterize the first propositions must itself have an initial certitude in its principle which guarantees all other certitudes or, rather, which is the form or essence of all certainty. In this sense, the primacy of mathematics points to a "metaphysics of subjectivity," i.e., a project basing knowledge on the certainty of the subject represented as the unique criterion of truth: "This mathematical requirement of certainty as the criterion of all knowledge finds a quite definite fulfillment historically. From this, it follows that the *ego cogito* is posited as what is first of all and truly knowable and thus *true*.... Descartes thus created the ground and foundation sufficient for *it* and placed knowledge in general upon the self-certainty of the principle: 'I think, I—am'" (*ST,* 30).

It is just this requirement of grounding the totality of knowledge on the certainty of the subject (the same locus where, as Strauss, following Heidegger, insists the classical thinkers would have preferred an "objective" basis) that is effected in the methodical idea of systematicity, for it requires that the multiplicity of fields of knowledge be deduced from the unity of principles of a rationality inherent in subjectivity.[42] Finally—and this highlights the ontological meaning of the notion of system—the subject's certainty, set up as the criterion of the truth for all knowledge, also becomes the criterion of being; only what accords with the subject's certitude may be considered as genuinely existing: "The self-certainty of thinking decides what 'is,' as a principle and thus fundamentally.... And only what is *true* can be acknowledged as truly *existent.* The self-certainty of thinking becomes the court of judgment which decides what can be *and cannot* be, even more, what *Being* means in general" (*ST,* 30–31).

As Alain Renaut shows, Heidegger's analysis—an analysis whose scope will be underestimated if we realize that what is described here under the name "metaphysics of subjectivity" definitely continues to outlive Hegel's completion of it, if only as the idea of a "science of history" implying an identification of the real with the rational—needs, however, to be supplemented insofar as it is limited to defining the project of systematicity common to German idealism as regards the primacy of mathematics. Now, as we have seen, we must also think of the notion of system as related to the organic: this necessity becomes clear when we note that, in a mathematical proof, the elements deduced from principles (theorems deduced from axioms) rest on the same foundation but are still not interconnected in a systematic or organic way. So if German idealism regards the totality of knowledge and being as an organized (and not simply mathematical) system, the reason is that the real is thought of not only as conformable to mathematics but also as life or as self-production.[43] Thus we see how in Hegel, the most representative figure of system, it is from a self-producing or self-engendering principle that we see the coherence of the multiple, and hence how this system can reconcile the theoretical and the practical, intelligence and will (self-production).

From this briefly sketched philosophical project[44] which seems to be common to German idealists, we may "deduce" the essence of its political project: if what is to be thought of is the system, i.e., the rationality of the real,[45] political thought may be merely a reflection of the conditions for actualizing that systematic rationality by or in the state. Hence the political question is essentially that of actualizing the system. This is easily seen in any analysis—bearing on the example of a then-central political question, that of the university—which I shall briefly recall here[46] for its paradigmatic value.

If the German idealists were concerned with any concrete political question, it was definitely that of the relation between the university and the state: in the space of barely fifteen years, from 1802 to 1816, Schelling, Fichte, Schleiermacher, Humboldt, and Hegel wrote about the university, proposing different plans of organization, and thus demonstrating, for a particular political question, an interest that is easily shown to be philosophically oriented.[47]

Indeed, what is a university? The very concept of university implies that the multiple turns toward unity, in other words, a systematic totalization of the multiple. At the conceptual level, as Heidegger was to recall again, the uni-versity requires "the rootedness of the sciences in their essential ground," the imposition from this ground of some "unity" to the "multiplicity of disciplines" that each study some field of reality.[48] In accordance with its concept, the university should institutionalize the systematic demands of philosophy, actualizing the philosophical as such. This was emphasized by Schelling: the university gets its name from the ideal of "the true organic life of [all parts of] knowledge" (*US,* 24), i.e , from the idea of system, and so it is a matter of questioning the real, the university's reality, using the idea of the system. The philosophical undertaking thus becomes clear: to require the real, and in particular the university, to be systematic; this becomes inevitable where the philosophical orientation is precisely that for which, at the theoretical level of the concept, "the particular has value only insofar as it implies the universal and absolute" (*US,* 6), in which the spirit of system reigns.

What a reading of texts suffices to show with certainty is that under these conditions the political project is to embody the idea of a system, as the works are all imbued with the spirit of what Schelling called "uni-totality":

- In his 1803 *On University Studies* Schelling asks, "What is the pivotal issue on which everything else turns?" The answer: "It is the idea of an intrinsically unconditioned knowledge, one and entire—the primordial knowledge, which in the phenomenal world exists only in separate branches, no longer as the one single great tree of knowledge"(9); i.e., the idea of "the organic whole of the sciences" (7) in the "universal rational knowledge which should be self-evident and transparent"(9), the idea of the "system."
- In his *Deductive Plan for a Higher Teaching Establishment to be Founded in Berlin* (§ 21) Fichte asks, What is "that toward which we are tending?" "The unity of the thing from a unique point of view"—i.e., the idea of a totality of knowledge in which each element is "an indispensable part of a greater totality," which must be "permeated by a clear concept" so that the parts "are interconnected" (§ 60).

In Schleiermacher and Humboldt, the idea of system, while more implicit, is just as dominant:

- In his *Thoughts on Universities of German Conception,* Schleiermacher asks, What is the presiding "point of view" at the organization of the university? That of "science in its idea," i.e., of science defined, as in Fichte or Hegel, as the encyclopedic viewpoint of the initial concatenation of the parts within the whole.
- In his *On the Internal and External Organization of Scientific Establishments in Berlin,* Humboldt asks, what will be the point of departure for the organization of teaching: "the principle of subdividing the higher scientific establishments and their different kinds"? This is called "the idea." What is this idea? Humboldt explains that it combines a principle and an ideal: the "original principle from which the scientific world attempts to 'derive everything,'" i.e., a unification from which everything should be "deduced"; the ideal of this derivation or deduction, the idea to which every effort must be related—the idea thus being the one of science itself, of a system as a requirement of the logical and complete deduction of the multiplicity from a unique and unifying principle.

—Finally, as we read Hegel[49], we are struck by the fact that everything he says about the gymnasium and university is based on the conviction that the system is complete, that under the name "philosophical encyclopedia" there exists "a systematic complex of the sciences"; from this comes "the requirement to form an ordered whole, constructed in all its parts, out of the vast field of objects belonging to philosophy," i.e., all the sciences, this is what the "new idea" of instruction should achieve.

This permanent return of a demand to embody "uni-totality" becomes clear when we put all its operations into the framework of philosophical thinking from Kant to Hegel: the creation of philosophy as a system. The political problem thus is located precisely in the space that connects, but also separates, the real (here, the university) and the ideal (the system), and it is this disparity that gives it its meaning. Measured against its conceptual requirements, what scene did the existing university present from Schelling to Hegel? Schelling: "It is at the very beginning of his university career that the young man first comes into contact with the world of science. The more taste and inclination he has for science, the more likely it is that this world will strike him as a chaos, a confused mass, a vast ocean upon which he is launched without star or compass" (*US*, 5). Fichte says that at a university where one learns only "fragments" of knowledge (§2), and this by an unorganized process governed by "the effect of chance," where education is determined solely by "good luck and chance" (§10), the absence of the encyclopedic outlook "throws the student without rudder or compass into a sea of confusion." (§21). Hegel in 1816: "It appears that the sciences we have preserved are maintained merely through tradition and a belief in their formal utility for the development of the understanding," an example being logic, which no one knows how to fit into the concept of a university.

Thus, the uni-versity as such does not exist—this is the diagnosis we find throughout their various texts: what prevails is not the university as a system, but seeming chaos Energy is wasted, for "at best, by the end of their academic career [students] are rewarded with insight into how fruitless their labors have been, ... how much they have learned to no purpose and how many essentials they have neglected" (*US*, 5–6). We repeat to the point of absurdity what has already been written in books—the university's transmission of knowledge thus looking like a "pedagogical practice of penury" (Fichte, *Deductive Plan*, §2); we claim to cultivate originality, "i.e., contingency, the arbitrary, peculiarity of opinion," before even giving opinion material to feed on—which is strictly incoherent, for obviously it is "only after his mind is filled with ideas that the student is capable of propelling himself further into the sciences and of achieving true originality" (Hegel, *On Teaching Philosophy at the Gymnasium/at the University*). So, we have an unsatisfactory reality, like a university with no apparent rules, principles, or concepts. A particularly disgraceful reality for those in whose theoretical work rationality is on the way to completion: in this sense, the political requirement that a university's reality measure up to its completed concept was perhaps "never more pressing than at the present time, when everything in science and art seems to be tending toward unity, when matters that long seemed remote from each other are now recognized to be quite close" (*US,* 7). At a time when philosophy meant working toward this completion of the system, the political question may only spring from the unacceptable disparity between the real and the rational, in this case the contradictions between the academic world and the systematic concept of a university.

Then it is indeed history—and Strauss's analysis proves relevant here—that appears to mediate between the real and the ideal. Furthermore, it may be asserted that under these conditions the philosophy of history forms the link that necessarily connects philosophy as thinking about the ideal of the system and politics as aiming at its embodiment. So in light of this brief analysis of a particular political, but certainly paradigmatic, question, it seems that Strauss's interpretation of modernity is wholly confirmed at the three levels we have considered: the speculative philosophy peculiar to German idealism seemed to have carried out the liquidation of Greek "objectivity," while establishing a humanist metaphysics in which subjectivity becomes the mistress of all knowledge and being; for political thought, then, the framework for reflection becomes the question of the actualization of the ideal which philosophy has defined as the universal system of the domination of the subject; finally, the task of spelling out the modalities of this actualization must be entrusted to the philosophy of history.

Let's take stock: up to now, there was an apparently simple connection between the allegiance to the theoretical project of systematicity and the reading of the university's reality as chaotic and confused, in short, as out of step with the aim of the completed system. The unanimity revealed in the observation of the disparity should entail a unanimous wish for reform (even for revolution) aiming to make the university adequate to the concept of a university, to what it rationally "ought to be." Now, it is precisely here—in the way of conceiving the transforming action—that the unanimity vanishes, the philosophers splitting into two opposed camps: one, if you will, liberal and reform-minded, made up of those who see the bringing together of the real and the ideal as a process both ineluctable and immanent in the real, in short, a process that is not imposed from the outside (in the name of the ideal). In this conception of history we clearly recognize the one that Strauss correctly calls "realism," a conception that, particularly in Schelling and Hegel, takes the form of a theory of the cunning of reason. The other "camp," in a sense more "authoritarian" but also more revolutionary—and in fact Fichte is its lone representative—sees the reconciliation of the ideal and the real as fundamentally unnecessary, i.e., depending simply on the freedom or "good will" of persons who decide to bring about the actualization of a political project, the success of which is not guaranteed by anything theoretical. In short, as we had foreseen, the tension in fact pervading what seemed to assume the form of a common philosophical and political project shows up most clearly at the level of the philosophy of history, and we also see that we now must literally reverse the opinion that German idealism is a basically univocal, although externally divided project.

Fichte's position thus seems to me immune from Strauss's analysis of modernity, for, without completely separating the real and the ideal—which remain linked by practical necessity—, he in no way suggests that their fusion is inevitable. Thus, none of Strauss's criteria of modernity—the identity of the rational and the real, realism, the priority of politics over ethics, the lowering of the goal, the suppression of transcendence, the superiority of freedom over reason—appears applicable to Fichte.[50] To suppose at this level a "complicity" between "utopian" thought and realism, a complicity that would allow for their reconciliation in Hegelianism, would amount to condemning the cardinal opposition clearly shown here as simply *apparent*. That would amount to—and on this point Manent's argument has the virtue of being unambiguous—considering Hegel's critique of the "moral view of the world" as legitimate and conclusive. Thus we clearly see that only at this cost can Strauss's hypothesis of a univocality of philosophies of the second wave be confirmed.

Because the ontological preconditions of Fichte's philosophy of history are examined the second book in the present series, I shall confine myself here to examining how Fichte intended to destroy, though without "leaving modernity," the speculative foundations of what Strauss called rationalistic historicism. More clearly perhaps, if rationalistic historicism has its philosophical basis in the assertion that rationality equals reality (so that ideality and reality necessarily coincide), we shall agree that any philosophy that denies some form of this identification is antihistoricist. As the reader can observe—no doubt with a certain surprise if he knows Fichte only through his textbook image—, the one and only purpose of the theoretical part of the *Science of Knowledge* is to lay bare the element of sophistry inherent in the philosophical position positing this identity (chapter three).

This critique of metaphysics shows how (chapter four), in the space thus opened up between reality and rationality, we may forge the project of a political philosophy creating a public space of intersubjectivity, i.e., a theory of rights that is modern (since it does not renounce subjectivity), and yet nonhistoricist.

The Preconditions for a Nonhistoricist Modernity: The Young Fichte

Fichte's Critique
of Metaphysics and the
Basis of Natural Right

As all commentators have noted, our understanding of the first *Science of Knowledge* runs into nearly insuperable difficulties. The most obvious problem—among many others—comes quite simply from the fact that the reader, even when familiar with the issues debated by German philosophers of the period, cannot grasp what Fichte is talking about in the book's first three paragraphs. There we find set forth, in formal and near-mathematical language, three principles whose meaning and philosophical interest are so unclear that for nearly two centuries[1] they have been as unintelligible to historians of philosophy as they were to Fichte's contemporaries.

The principles are:

1) "self = self" (usually wrongly interpreted as the veridical grasp of an absolute self containing all reality);
2) "self ≠ not-self" (positing of the world, of the object-in-itself);
3) "In the self, the self opposes a divisible not-self to the divisible self" (an attempt to reconcile subject and object within the absolute self metaphysically conceived as the substrate of this division).

Let the nonphilosopher be reassured: I am not about to give a "technical" commentary on these three propositions: I would simply like to show how, beyond their speculative dryness, they set up issues that, despite appearances, have a direct bearing on our topic (the search for the preconditions for a philosophy of natural right that is modern, i.e., upholding the ideas of reason and free will, but still altogether antihistoricist). Fichte's goal was a philosophical critique of two speculative denials of the existence of natural (ideal) right as distinct from positive (actual) right, i.e., two forms of radical historicism.

The foregoing discussion has shown that—and here Strauss's arguments are irreproachable—by asserting the identity of the rational and the real, rationalist metaphysics concludes that political philosophy is impossible. Now, Fichte saw two philosophical ways to produce this identity:

- Idealism begins with the subject and argues that, outside representation, the object, the real, not only does not exist (see Berkeley) but also is fully consistent with and identical to the logical (ontological) principles of subjectivity, in particular the principle of sufficient reason (Leibniz).
- Realism starts, by contrast, with the object in itself to show that the subject's representation is merely a reflection of this in-itself, and thoughts merely effects caused by an external reality (Spinoza).

We see in these two philosophies what Strauss—and Fichte would surely have agreed—considered the denial of the ultimate precondition of natural right, for in idealism the real reduces to the ideal, and in realism the ideal reduces to the real.

Thus, despite appearances, we are at the heart of our question right from the beginning of the *Science of Knowledge,* for the project, perhaps the most radical in modernity, is set up to undermine rationalist historicism right down to its very foundations.

Without needlessly going into the details of Fichte's text, we should indicate the meaning of these three first principles. As I have already suggested, the interpreter's difficulty stems from the fact that Fichte did nothing to make his meaning clear. The reason for this is, as Alexis Philonenko has carefully established, (1) that Fichte was assuming his reader had a perfect understanding of Kant's *Critique of Pure Reason,* notably the "Transcendental Dialectic" with its critique of dogmatic metaphysics, and (2) that Fichte goes through a systematic reconstruction of this transcendental dialectic using an approach that is the reverse of Kant's. So I shall try to make the meaning of this reconstruction clear before coming back to the properly existential stakes of this critique of historicism.

Continuing to take a very general view,[2] we may say that the *Critique of Pure Reason* follows a natural method in the sense that it proceeds from the true to the false. In the "Transcendental Aesthetic," Kant begins by asserting the first and most basic truth: the radical finiteness of the subject, defined by the fact that its capacity for knowledge is a priori "receptive," i.e., affected with an unalterable passivity: for awareness of subjectivity to exist, existence must be "given." So existence can never be dialectically deduced from the (the subject's) concept as being its other, for here otherness is irreducible. The "Aesthetic" thus sets forth the truth that makes metaphysics, as an ontological argument (the attempt to go from the subject, or the concept, to existence), into a logic of appearance (a "dialectics"). On the basis of this first truth, it becomes possible, in the "Transcendental Analytic," to approach the study of the structures of objectivity (deduction of categories and schematism) and thus to reach the second truth: scientific truth. Together, the "Aesthetic" and the "Analytic" thus constitute the totality of truth insofar as they are the true theory of the givenness of existence (of manifestation) and the adequate idea of the object's essence or quiddity. Only then does it become possible to approach the "Dialectic," i.e., the critique of the metaphysical error of identifying essence and manifestation (existence) by deducing the latter from the former. The *Critique of Pure Reason* thus proceeds from the true to the false, from the categories to Ideas, from the "Analytic" to the "Dialectic."

We should note, however, that Kant himself seems to suggest a reverse approach: we know that for him the "Transcendental Dialectic" (and in particular the antinomies) in turn shows the truth of the "Analytic." The *Critique of Pure Reason* mentions two types of proof:

- a direct proof by transcendental analysis, which we could call proof through the awareness of impossibility. It takes the notion of possible experience and shows that to conceive of experience, certain conditions must be admitted (intuitions, categories, schemata, principles);
- an indirect proof, provided by the "Transcendental Dialectic," which brings out to someone who would not admit the conditions revealed by the "Aesthetic" and the "Ana-

lytic" that their negation is a source of error or, more exactly, that it is the very source of the transcendental illusion.

Fichte adopted the second method, not the first. He thus begins with the false (of the "Dialectic") and proceeds to the true by a deconstruction and progressive reduction of error. Fichte begins the *Science of Knowledge* with a "Transcendental Dialectic" in order to return progressively to the schematism, then to a deduction of space and time, and finally to the very matter of sensation. Only at this point was the "Copernican Revolution" concluded and, correspondingly, as we shall see, the deconstruction of realism and idealism.

We shall further remark that, however unlike it is to Kant's, this approach stays within the framework of critical philosophy. Indeed, Fichte never claimed to be doing anything more than giving Kantian philosophy a systematic form. What he meant to renew in Kantianism was just the defects owing to the imperfection of the exposition.[3] So we may connect Fichte's method with Kant's in two ways:

- First, we may bring out (and this argument has a certain importance in questioning the systematic form of a philosophy, and hence the legitimacy of its starting point) that the transcendental illusion is a beginning that a Kantian would not find arbitrary, for Kant himself saw the illusion as necessary.
- We may think (and this falls under the heading of an improvement in the metaphysical deduction of the categories) that if it is possible to go from the categories to the Ideas, then, conversely, it must be possible to go from the Ideas to the categories by deconstructing the Ideas. Fichte thus starts with the Kantian notion that metaphysics contains everything, if only in the mode of illusion, or, if you like, from negation (the negation of temporality, negation of the difference between essence and existence, and so forth). Thus, the critique of metaphysics should indicate whatever truth is contained in it. If metaphysics is forgetfulness, abstraction from the difference between subject and object, between Being and thought—in a word, finiteness—, the critique of metaphysics may be presented, to

use Adorno's vocabulary, as a "negative dialectics," meaning a reparation or restoration of what was eliminated in the totalizing process of metaphysics.[4] The advantage of this method is clear: because metaphysics is systematic, so must the critique of it be. Therefore, philosophy, at least the theoretical part of it, essentially reduces to a *Dialectic,* meaning, as Kant did, not only a recreation of appearance but also a deconstruction of appearance.[5]

As Alexis Philonenko has shown,[6] Fichte started not with the absolute self (first principle) veridically reached through an "intellectual illusion" but with the absolute self as a transcendental illusion, i.e., from what Kant called a paralogism of pure reason. I will not go over Philonenko's numerous and irrefutable arguments in support of this thesis, but shall limit myself to picking out its implications for our inquiry.

—The first concerns the fact that because the absolute self is posited as an Idea, as an illusion and not a being in itself reached by an "intellectual intuition," it does not really eliminate the finite subject, as it necessarily would if its grasp were veridical. This remark is extremely important for our understanding of Fichte's method in the *Science of Knowledge.* It means that the philosopher's (the finite subject's) reflection may go on existing after the first principle, precisely because the illusory nature of the first principle does not negate finiteness. The whole dialectic rests on this initial cleavage between the philosophizing subject and the absolute self, which, being absolute, denies the finite subject, but because it is a merely illusory absolute lets it go on existing despite everything. "Reflection is free": the philosopher may start, and carry through as he sees fit, the work of deconstructing the illusion.

—At this very point, Hegel's reading of Fichte breaks down. Thinking that Fichte does indeed start with the absolute, Hegel criticizes him for the inconsistency[7] of positing a second principle (a reality external to the self) after the first, when reflection should have ceased. Hegel argued that Fichte could carry out his "deduction" only by making two errors: (a) the error of any "philosophy of reflection," which is to talk about the "thing in itself" from the outside instead of leaving it to its free development; (b) the error of starting with the absolute and introducing "the multiple" (the finite or the real) not by a deduction, but quite simply in an empirical way, because the philosophizing self knows that the external world exists.

This criticism, which would be valid if Fichte's philosophy began, as Hegel believed, with a Kantian "intellectual intuition",[8] i.e., with a veridical grasp of the absolute, is invalidated when we realize that Fichte's principles have their source not in the truth but in a dialectics of illusion that, by definition, lets the critical finite subject continue to exist.

These remarks may clarify the meaning of the first two principles. When the first principle positing the absolute self is taken as a "paralogism," as an illusion, then by thinking about the preconditions that make this positing possible—thinking that is wholly legitimate if we admit that the starting point is not truth but illusion—, we should get in the second principle the assertion of an absolute not-self. As Philonenko has written, "thus the transition from the self to the not-self comes about at the level of the presuppositions that require the constructions of the two first principles" (*LH,* 162). Once posited, the two terms formed by the self and the not-self are absolutely opposed, so we must reconcile them by admitting a third, synthetic principle: "In the self, the self opposes a divisible not-self to the divisible self."

I do not propose to make a detailed analysis of the structure of Fichte's dialectics, nor how it systematically articulates the different steps of Kant's "Transcendental Dialectic."[9] I would merely like to show how, from these three principles, Fichte sets forth the two philosophical positions—realism and idealism—criticized in the theoretical part of the *Science of Knowledge.* I shall briefly indicate how the self and the not-self are opposed in an antinomy that can be formulated from two points of view:

- From a strictly logical point of view, it follows that positing a not-self is absolutely incompatible with positing an absolute self that claims to be the totality of the real—the problem once again being that it is impossible to posit the one without the other, for they are based on logical constructions that are strictly parallel.
- But if we refer this opposition to the history of philosophy, Fichte is posing the classic problem of representation

whose critical formulation we find in Kant (in his *Letter to Markus Herz* of 21 February 1772) and whose skeptical formulation we find in Berkeley: how can I successfully posit something outside myself when this something by definition always remains an in-itself only *for me*,[10] and thus is never an in-itself genuinely external to me. Dogmatic realism (asserting the existence in itself of the not-self) always presupposes an element of negation of the self, i.e., the positing of an in-itself that does not exist for me, even though it is still the self that posited that this in-itself did not exist for it. Thus it is always *for the self* that the in-itself is asserted to not be for the self, the dogmatic assertion necessarily forgetting the first "for me" and thus falling into a pure contradiction: "the realist hypothesis, that the material of representation might be given to us somehow from without, admittedly made its appearance in the course of our investigation, . . . but on closer examination we found that such a hypothesis would contradict the principle proposed, since that to which a material was given from without would be no self at all, as it was required to be, but a not-self" (*SK*, 197) since the in-itself cannot be both in itself and for itself[11]

This obviously does not mean that Fichte accepts the "idealist" solution of the pure and simple negation of the not-self: it should be stressed that the two terms posited must be posited necessarily, for, because each presupposes the other, they reciprocally imply each other,[12] and so the simple juxtaposition of the two first principles creates an "analytic" opposition, i.e., a logical contradiction. Because, however, both these principles are in other respects "certain" (from the viewpoint of the formal logic "used as an organon"), they still have to be reconciled, just as (leaving the strictly logical terrain for that of the classic questions of the history of philosophy) we have to solve the problem of representation.

The difficulty in Fichte's thinking here is the following: we have seen that the two principles are opposed in a contradictory or analytical way.[13] From the viewpoint of formal logic they must be unreconcilable, for an absolute contradiction necessarily suggests the principle of the excluded middle. If Fichte judges that the two principles must be synthetically reconcilable in a third one, the reason must be that he is implicitly think-ing that this analytic contradiction is merely apparent and in fact conceals a synthetic opposition; which indisputably con-firms, if proof were needed, the correctness of Philonenko's thesis that the first three principles of the *Science of Knowledge* set forth a dialectical logic of appearance. To be persuaded of this, we need to recall what an "antinomy" is for Kant. An anti-nomy is an opposition between two theses that appear to be contradictory—hence, having the form of an opposition that suggests the principle of the excluded middle such that one proposition seems to have to be true and the other false—though in actuality the opposition is merely between contrar-ies or subcontraries. Thus, in the *Critique of Pure Reason,* the first two antinomies are oppositions of contraries (opposite in the same kind) so that both the thesis and the antithesis may be just apparently false, suggesting the excluded middle; for ex-ample, the world is neither finite nor infinite, and the alterna-tive is not exclusive, for it can be thought of as indefinite. In the third and fourth antinomies, the solution is the reverse, for it is a matter of subcontraries (the subject is understood in different senses in the thesis and the antithesis): in the third antinomy, for example, where the thesis considers man as noumenon and the antithesis as phenomenon, the two seemingly contradic-tory propositions may both be true provided we specify the meaning of the subject.

Thus, the opposition between the two first principles ap-pears to be an antinomy (of idealism and of realism). It is there-fore a matter of "composing" them, i.e., as in Kant, converting what seems at the level of illusion to be a logical contradiction into a transcendental opposition, so that we may interpret the transition from the first principle to the second as "the transi-tion of the paralogisms and their synthesis in an absolute self to the antinomy of representation" (*LH,* 164), and it is precisely this antithesis that the third principle—which thus corre-sponds to the expression of the critical solution[14] of an anti-nomy—is supposed to compose synthetically. This composi-tion will thus be the solution to the problem of the representation, for it reconciles idealism and realism which are the philosophical positions underlying the two first principles. Before we approach the sense of this critique of metaphysics, however, we need to see how it works in the third principle.

Starting with the illusion of the absolute self (first principle), we should also admit a second principle that, combined with the first, gives rise to an antinomy (an opposition that seems to be contradictory) whose real significance is the problem of representation (how can I admit the existence of something outside myself?). The problem whose third principle must indicate the solution may be expressed in the following way: it is a matter of transforming a merely apparent analytic contradiction into a genuine synthetic opposition. As Philonenko indicates, such a problem presupposes that three requirements are met: "In the first place, the two opposed terms must be opposed not only qualitatively (self and not-self, red and not red), but also quantitatively; the idea of quantity forms the basis of thinkable oppositions. Second, the quantitative opposition must have a qualitative significance; otherwise, the opposed terms could be thought to have the same sign and thus be additive. Lastly, the third requirement: if the opposition keeps a qualitative meaning, then the two opposites combined must compose the same whole" (*LH,* 166). Thus, to be thinkable, the opposition must become quantitative: the two terms are opposed not absolutely but only in part. Hence the idea of a "divisible" self and of a divisible "not-self," i.e., the two terms into which reality is divided. What enables us to think this opposition has a qualitative sense (so that the two terms continue to be opposed, not being additive) is the introduction of the concept of negative magnitude that grounds the idea of reciprocal action: the self and the not-self divide the totality of the real, their opposite quantities maintaining a relation of reciprocity, as in a system of forces. This totality is none other than that of the absolute self that still remains the substrate of the division between the finite self and the finite not-self; hence the formulation of the third principle: "In the self I oppose a divisible not-self to the divisible self" (*SK,* 110).

To make the developments in the following two chapters intelligible, I make two observations: (1) we should keep firmly in mind the idea that the principles stated at the beginning of the *Science of Knowledge* are *all* false (not just the first one); as Philonenko has suggested,[15] they may justly be compared to the three metaphysical ideas criticized by Kant in the "Transcendental Dialectic." The first principle corresponds to the Idea of an absolute individual self (a psychological Idea), the second to the Idea of an absolute not-self, i.e., of a world in itself (a cosmological idea), and the third to the divine synthesis of the subject in itself and of the object in itself. (2) Because the subject in itself and the object in itself are within the illusion, radically cut off from each other, the deconstruction of metaphysics will have the Kantian sense of a "refutation of idealism": its only aim will be to show how the subject and the object must be *both* connected and separated (which is believed by metaphysicians who manage only to reduce one to the other, be it idealistically in bringing the subject to the object—to its simple reflection). The deconstruction of the illusion will thus lead man back to his own truth, which Fichte formulates as follows: "as soon as you come to be clear about your philosophy, this illusion [of a thing in itself] will fall from your eyes like scales. . . . You will then claim to know no more in life than that you are finite, and finite in *this particular way,* which you are obliged to account for by the presence of *that sort of world* outside you; and you will no more be minded to overstep these bounds than you are to cease being yourself" (*SK,* 82).

Reading this text, one is hard put to understand how Fichte could be so long considered a champion of "subjective idealism," for his only aim was to remind man of his finiteness by connecting his awareness with that of a world. The reason for this, however, may be indicated, and it is one of considerable methodological importance: thinking that Fichte started from the truth, from an authentic grasp of the absolute self, interpreters could see—in the deduction performed in the *Science of Knowledge*—forms not only of sensibility but also of their matter—only a radical idealism. If, on the contrary, we admit that Fichte is starting with illusion, this deduction immediately takes on exactly the opposite meaning; we can say that in a certain way the absolute self contains all reality, but we then must understand that it is in a purely negative mode. If the absolute self includes all reality, its claim to eternal self-sufficiency as an absolute entails a denial of the external world and temporality, as already indicated in Kant's "Transcendental Dialectic." Therefore, Fichte's approach is essentially "reparative," presenting a purely negative dialectics in which the deconstruction of illusion restores what was eliminated by the illusion's claim to absoluteness, i.e., the external world and the finite subject located in time. In this sense, Fichte's dialectics is from first to last a critique of metaphysical illusion, and it is only such a critique that may give rise to a truth that did not preexist it. As such, it immediately possesses a "political" significance since, condemning the elimination of the finite subject in all its forms, it sets forth the theoretical preconditions for an area of intersubjectivity.

Thus, there is room to establish a rigorous connection between the critique of the metaphysical foundations of historicism (the confusion of the ideal and the real in idealism and realism) and the possibility of a modern political philosophy: if the political philosophy, as Strauss rightly says, presupposes the possibility of a critique of positivity, it is clear that this possibility is dismissed in idealism and realism which, each for opposite reasons, can think of history as subject to necessity only. For there to be a critique of positivity, the subject and the world must be both distinguished and nevertheless thought of in relation to each other.[16] Either a separation or total union of the two terms makes the very idea of critique irretrievably lose all meaning, and without it, as Strauss concedes, we cannot conceive, in whatever mode, the opposition between natural right and positive right.

The next chapters will thus be devoted to (1) an examination of Fichte's critique of the metaphysical foundations of historicism and (2) an argument that this critique opens up an area in which a political philosophy becomes thinkable and still remains modern in that it does not give up this subjectivity (humanism) whose metaphysical fate (historicism) it managed to show was not inevitable.

The Antinomy of Realism and Idealism: The Deconstruction of the Ontological Bases of Historicism

I propose here to analyze the antinomial opposition between realism and idealism as set forth by Fichte in points A, B, C, D, and E of §4 in the *Science of Knowledge*. Given that I shall not be explaining the meaning of these texts but merely showing how they form the basis of a critical idea of metaphysical illusions and a certain conception of rights, I shall confine myself to the definitive formulation of the antinomy in point E and disregard the dialectical process leading up to it.[1]

1. Dialectics as the Creation and Deconstruction of Illusions

In C, realism is defined as positing that "the not-self has reality for the self only to the extent that the self is affected" (*SK*, 130). This positing corresponds to the principle of causality or efficacy: by observing the self's passivity, we conclude, from the concept of reciprocal action derived from the third principle, in favor of an activity in the not-self (which is equal to the self's passivity). Thus, it is by being affected that we posit causality in the not-self, which amounts to indicating the vector, or, if you will, the order in which to read the reciprocal determination between the self and the not-self: for realism, we have to go from the not-self to the self, from the not-self's activity to the self's passivity. Thus, according to realism, "negation or passivity must be posited in the self, and by the rule of interdetermination in general, the same quantum of reality or activity in the not-self" (*SK*, 138–39). We can say that in this sense being affected is the *ratio cognoscendi* of the not-self's activity and that the latter is the *ratio essendi* of the self's passivity.

It should be noted that this definition of realism is to some extent a critical definition, for from the affected subject it infers the existence of its active object (the not-self). In Spinozistic terms, we can say that the reality of the substance (of the not-self) is posited from the mode (of the finite subject), the not-self appearing as a construction for explaining, but, once again, from the mode, the affection it perceives in itself.

Now, according to Fichte, "these answers have taken us winging in a circle" (*SK,* 139), i.e., an internal contradiction that necessarily (antinomially) causes realism surreptitiously to adopt the opposing principle: idealism.

Fichte describes the circle this way:

> Assume, as the first case under the pure concept of efficacy, that the limitation of the self arises wholly and solely from the activity of the not-self. Suppose that, at time A, the not-self is not operating on the self, so that all reality and no negation at all is posited in the self, and hence, by the foregoing, that no reality is posited in the not-self. Suppose further, that at time B the not-self operates with three degrees of activity on the self, so that in virtue of the concept of indetermination, three degrees of reality are abolished in the self, and three degrees of negation posited in their stead. But here the self merely behaves passively: the degrees of negation are posited, indeed, but they *are* merely *posited—for some intelligent being* external to the self, which observes the self and not-self engaged in this transaction, and judges by the rules of indetermination; but not *for the self as such.* The latter would require that it should be able to compare its state at time A with that at time B, and to distinguish the different quanta of its activity at both times; and we have not yet shown how this is possible. In the case supposed, the self would certainly be limited, but it would not be aware of its limitation. (*SK,* 139–40)

The principle of the refutation of realism is thus the following: for the not-self to be posited as the cause of the affection, the "mode" first has to be aware of itself, positing itself as passive and positing its passivity; in short, being active and passive at the same time. Nevertheless, according to realism, the self is purely passive in this operation. Thus the mode is limited by substance uniquely for the thinking of the philosopher describing the operation: it is the philosopher who, through his own thinking, gives rise to the self-awareness of the observed mode and actively posits this mode as passive. Now this problem is insoluble, for by this very description, the philosopher is also a mode, affected by another mode he is describing. Under these conditions, what reason has the philosopher to posit himself as actively positing the mode as passive? Here we are clearly ensnared in an infinite regress: if the not-self's activity may be posited only from the self's awareness of its being affected, then the affected self has to perceive this affection: for if it is perceived by an external observer, the same question immediately arises: how could it perceive itself as affected by what it is observing?

Philonenko neatly summarizes this difficulty: "In the *Ethics* self-awareness is surreptitiously introduced by the relation of the philosopher to the mode; affected by the thought of the affection of the mode, the philosopher takes the place of the self-awareness of the mode. He is really merely a consciousness of the object for another awareness of the object. The awareness of the self is a pure appearance, and, in principle, one never transcends object-awareness. The natural result is an utter inability to solve the problem of intentionality." (*LH*, 205). We see that Fichte's demonstration results in this point: we may legitimately posit the not-self's action on the self only if we start from the awareness of the self as affected. Here Fichte again finds the profound meaning of Kant's "Refutation of Idealism" in his *Critique of Pure Reason:* we can think properly about intentionality only if we indissolubly connect object-awareness and self-awareness, realism and idealism. Fichte's main criticism of Spinoza is that he must deny self-awareness in favor of object-awareness: "He separates *pure* and *empirical* consciousness. The first he attributes to God, who is never conscious of himself, since pure consciousness never attains to consciousness; the second he locates in the specific modifications of the Deity. So established, his system is perfectly consistent and irrefutable, since he takes his stand in a territory where reason can no longer follow him; but it is also groundless; for what right did he have to go beyond the pure consciousness given in empirical consciousness" (*SK*, 101)?

Spinozism not only must posit self-awareness (since the not-self can be asserted only from the awareness of being affected) but also must deny self-awareness in object-awareness, never then managing to connect self-awareness with object-awareness. For Fichte, Spinozism involved both an error and a lack: not thinking his own thought,[2] the dogmatic thinker is led to "transcend the self" (*SK*, 118), to posit identity as being and not as duty:

> There would ... be absolutely no explaining how any thinker should ever have been able to go beyond the self, or how, having once done so, he could ever have come to a standstill, if we did not encounter a practical datum which completely accounts for this phenomenon. . . .
> It is easy enough to see what impelled [Spinoza] to his system, namely the necessary endeavor to bring about the highest unity in human

> cognition. This unity is present in his system, and the error of it is merely that he thought to deduce on grounds of theoretical reason what he was driven to merely by a practical need; that he claimed to have established something as truly given, when he was merely setting up an appointed, but never attainable, ideal. (*SK*, 118, 101)

For it is uniquely as a practical ideal actualizable in history that the absolute self may remain present in the finite self and that the limits of criticism cannot be transgressed. Realism thus leads to idealism because it necessarily must postulate, without ever being able to realize idealism's principle, namely, self-awareness.

The self, as awareness of the self and the object, must at the same time be posited as active and passive: this is the formulation of the problem of representation which was inherited, as it were, by idealism, which repeats the question as the failure of realism left it. To get rid of this contradiction, idealism must eliminate the passivity that creates a problem from the viewpoint of self-awareness. In the Leibnizian tradition, this reduction of passivity is brought about by the principle of continuity through an operation that Salomon Maimon first described within the framework of Kantian philosophy. Given that it is essentially Maimon who is aimed at here, we should recall his solution of the question[3] in the second section of the *Versuch über die Transcendentalphilosophie*.[4]

Like all post-Kantians, Maimon dealt with Kant's formulation of the problem of representation by trying to rule out the existence of the thing in itself. This question thus touches on the one that Fichte asks in this text, because for Maimon ruling out the thing in itself is equivalent to the deduction of the passivity of representation based on the very spontaneity of the understanding. This operation is effected by a return to Leibniz's infinitesimal calculus and the principle of continuity: just as for Leibniz (unlike Descartes), rest is merely a limiting case of the subject's activity (one goes from movement to rest by the principle of continuity), Maïmon tries to conceive of passivity (receptivity of the sensibility that creates the still realist and dogmatic hypothesis of the thing in itself) as a limiting case of the subject's activity, or, to use Maimon's mathematical language, as a "differential of spontaneity": "What is empirical in intuitions (matter) is really given, like light rays, by something external to us (hence distinct from us). But we should not be troubled by the expression 'external to us' as if it were a thing with some spatial relation to us; this external to us means simply this: a thing in whose representation we are not aware of any spontaneity, i.e., from the viewpoint of our awareness, a state of pure and simple passivity in us, a state in which there is no activity on our part."[5]

The notion of externality thus leads back to that of passivity, and that of passivity to a limiting case of the self's activity (by reference to the principle of continuity): by modifying Kant's concept of infinite understanding, the finite (passive) understanding is conceived of as a limiting case of the activity of the infinite understanding which, by making itself finite, produces the given as passivity, as the differential of two activities: "Reason demands that we consider the given in an object, not as something immutable by nature, but as a result of the limitation in our ability to know which would disappear in an infinitely superior intellect. Reason thus seeks an infinite progression by which what is thought is always increased, and what is given, decreased, to the infinitesimal."[6] Here we see how Maimon modifies Kant's thought: no doubt Kant thought of the progress of knowledge as the progress of the finite understanding toward infinite understanding that ideally tends to reduce the share of the given in favor of the known. For Kant, however, this obviously involves an unreachable ideal, for the two understandings are radically disconnected,[7] the sign of this disconnection being precisely the passivity of the sensibility. In Maimon, on the other hand, we must think of the possibility of a transition between these two understandings, so as to deduce this passivity and also to eliminate the necessity to explain affection by the external thing in itself.

This transition will be effected through a Leibnizian reinterpretation of Kant's argument concerning "anticipations of perception"; Kant says that it is possible to "anticipate" something a priori of the real, i.e., the fact that it has a degree. This is no doubt one of the points where Kant most closely approaches "idealism," for he admits the possibility of determining a priori the empirically real, not only its form but also its content:

> All knowledge by means of which I am enabled to know and determine a priori what belongs to empirical knowledge may be entitled an anticipation.... But as there is an element in the appearances (namely, sensation, the matter of perception) which can never be known a priori, and which therefore constitutes the distinctive difference between empirical and a priori knowledge, it follows that sensation is just that element which cannot be anticipated.... If, however, there is in every sensation, as sensation in general, ... something that can be known a priori, this will, in a quite especial sense, deserve to be named anticipation. For it does indeed seem surprising that we

> should forestall experience, precisely in that which concerns what is only to be obtained through it, namely, its matter. Yet, none the less such is actually the case.[8]

What is anticipated is the fact that sensation has a degree, a magnitude of intensity, and thus that it must be thought of as a summation (whole) of the infinitely small. Kant's proof of this may be summarized as follows:

- Between a 0 degree of awareness and an Nth degree (appearance of the clear awareness), there is time.
- Now, because time is divisible into infinitely small units, there is an infinite number of infinitely small instants between 0 and N.
- Therefore, when our full awareness appears, there has already been an infinity of states of least awareness going from total unconsciousness (0 degree) to the full empirical awareness (N).[9]

Though it stays within the limits of criticism, this proof opens two areas into which idealism may enter.

(a) First, it reduces the share of the given in favor of that of the a priori: the Nth degree is produced not by the external thing in itself but by the subject's (the imagination's) activity which synthesizes (in a whole) degrees of infinitesimal awareness to the threshold N. Compared with the "Transcendental Aesthetic," the role of externality is thus reduced relative to that of the subject.

(b) Next, Kant sometimes seems to describe this process as a trajectory going from the pure self to the empirical subject: "[F]rom empirical consciousness to pure consciousness a graduated transition is possible, the real in the former completely vanishing and a merely formal a priori consciousness of the manifold in space and time remaining. Consequently there is also possible a synthesis in the process of generating the magnitude of a sensation from its beginning in pure intuition = 0, up to any required magnitude."[10]

This text, which may, despite appearances, still be interpreted within the limits of criticism,[11] nevertheless suggests the idea that the empirical awareness would be produced by the transition to the limit of pure awareness: all Maimon had to do was indicate that the infinitely small units that the imagination integrates to produce the Nth degree result not from something in itself but from a transition in the limit of pure awareness, a finitization of the infinite understanding, so that what is an integral for the finite understanding is a derivative for the infinite understanding, which Maimon can formulate as follows: "Thus, the sensibility provides the differentials for a determinate awareness; the imagination draws from them a determinate finite object of intuition; the understanding extracts from the relation between these various differentials that are objects the relation of sensory objects that come from them." [12] Let us comment briefly on this text:

- The sensibility provides differentials: in sensibility we find differentials by the transition to the limit of pure awareness.
- The imagination puts them in the form of an intuition (the Nth degree).
- Finally, as in Kant, the understanding compares and assembles the intuitions to make specific objects of them. [13]

This solves the problem of passivity: passivity is nothing, or, more exactly, it is only a differential of activity, an infinitely small thing that, as such, does not require an explanation referring to a thing in itself external to the subject. This is the idealist solution that, contrary to one received idea, Fichte criticizes as being as illusory as that of realism.

Let us reformulate Maimon's solution in Fichte's language: in relation to a quantum that is the totality of reality (since one starts with the absolute self) or of activity, passivity is nothing positive, but simply the difference between a total activity and a partial activity, so that in itself, being absolutely nothing, passivity does not need to be explained: "Now in the self reality is posited. And thereby the self must be posited an *absolute totality* of the real (which is to say, as a quantum in which all others are contained, and which can serve as a measure for all of them). . . . By reference to this absolutely posited standard, the amount of a want of reality (a passivity) is to be determined. But the want is nothing, and nor is that which wants" (*SK*, 132).

This solution traps us in a circle that is symmetrical to the one of realism. The difficulty lies in conceiving of this limitation of the self without referring to the dogmatic not-self. Now, this is impossible:

[S]uppose, as the second case under the pure concept of substantiality, that the self should have an absolute power, independent of any influence from the not-self, of positing arbitrarily a diminished quantum of reality in itself; the presupposition of transcendental idealism, and in particular of the preestablished harmony, which is an idealism of this

> type. Here we abstract entirely from the fact that this presupposition already contradicts our absolute first principle. Grant further that the self has the power of comparing this diminished quantity with absolute totality, and of measuring it thereby. Suppose, on these terms, that at time A the self has two degrees of diminished activity, and at time B, three. It can then be easily understood how the self could judge itself to be limited at both times, and to be more limited at time B than at time A. But there is no seeing at all how this limitation could be related to anything in the not-self as its cause. For the self would be obliged, rather, to regard itself as the cause thereof (*SK*, 140).

Therefore, the problem with idealism is the reverse of the problem with Spinozism: if the self is mere self-awareness, we cannot see how, from the comparison of a quantum of activity X with a quantum of a lesser activity Y, it may refer the limitation (the difference between these two quanta) to something external to it: rather, it should perceive the limit *in it*.

Fichte's argument may startle us if we do not realize that, despite appearances, his criticism of dogmatic idealism is an internal criticism; despite appearances: for it may seem odd that one needs idealism to refer the limitation to a not-self when its essence is the denial of the not-self. To grasp Fichte's maneuver, we thus need to stress that even if dogmatic idealism denies all not-self external to representation, it must explain on its own ground (i.e., without leaving the self, the sphere of representation) the very phenomenon of intentionality which, as subjective experience, is not dubitable: "The justification for this relation to a not-self is, indeed, denied by the dogmatic idealist, and to that extent he is consistent: but he cannot deny the fact of relation, nor has it occurred to anyone to do so. But then he at least has to explain this admitted fact, as distinct from its justification" (*SK*, 140). Now, dogmatic idealism cannot explain the phenomenon of intentionality (once again, it would only be to condemn it), for we do not understand why the empirical self would subjectively experience an internal limitation on the self (a difference between two degrees of activity) as a relation of externality to a not-self, so that dogmatic idealism is doubly absurd. First, it starts with a hypothesis (the limitation of the self which was admitted simply to see what flowed from it) that contradicts its own essence: we do not understand the source of the self's limitation: if the self is defined as the absolute quantum of activity, why and how would it be limited if it is not constrained by a not-self? And how could it be prevented from doing so by a not-self if it is the absolute totality of the activity?

> *If* the self posits a lesser degree of activity in itself, then it admittedly posits thereby a passivity in itself and an activity in the not-self. But the self can have no power to posit absolutely a lower degree of activity in itself; for in virtue of the concept of substantiality, it posits all activity, and nothing but activity, in itself. Hence the positing of this lower degree of activity in the self would have to be preceded by an activity of the not-self. . . . But this is impossible, in that, owing to the concept of efficacy, the not-self can be credited with an activity only to the extent that a passivity is asserted in the self (*SK,* 139).

Dogmatic idealism therefore starts with an absurd hypothesis, and, in a second absurdity, this costly hypothesis proves to be pointless, for, as we have seen, it does not succeed in explaining what is in question: intentionality.

To ground itself, dogmatic idealism is thus forced to appeal to the opposing principle and to refer surreptitiously to the idea of a causality foreign to the monad. Hence, the antinomial character of the opposition between realism and idealism: to justify themselves, thesis and antithesis each refer to the opposing principle they are intended to refute. Spinozism must presuppose self-consciousness, of affection or passivity, in order to justify the positing of causality in the not-self. Now it can only postulate this self-consciousness and never explain it, except by an altogether unilluminating infinite regress. For its part, idealism, even one admitting the hypothesis of a limitation of activity with the monadic absolute self, since it cannot refer this limitation to a not-self, cannot explain intentionality. As Philonenko has written, in idealism "it is self-consciousness that now appears cut off from object-consciousness. Only the philosopher reflecting from the outside on the self's or monad's activity can assert that the self's spontaneous modification by itself corresponds to a real external modification, so that, grasped from the outside, the self-consciousness of the self is an object-consciousness. The self, the monad, is always for itself a self-consciousness—it is the philosopher who posits it at the same time as an object-consciousness" (*LH,* 204). Hence, the converse error symmetrical to that of realism.

It is not my intention here to indicate Fichte's solution to this antinomy.[14] I do, however, insist that it is outrageous to reduce his solution to the pure and simple reassertion of dogmatic idealism in such a way as to assimilate his philosophy to this position, for the whole theoretical part of the *Science of Knowledge* is a refutation of it. We next remark that this critique of metaphysical illusion may in certain respects provide the model for a critique of political ideologies, a critique characterizable by the terms defetishization, reparation, and communication.

2. The Criticist Critique of Metaphysics as a Model for a Theory of Ideologies

—Defetishization, for the distinguishing property of metaphysical illusion, for both realism and idealism, is not to call the philosopher's positing into question: he takes the place of the mode's self-awareness or the monad's object-awareness without the possibility of this operation being even conceived of; neither is it clear how the philosopher, who is a mode or a monad himself, can avoid the limitation inherent in the object under study. In short, the metaphysician is not thinking his own thought, so that he produces a purely objective system with no concern for questioning the subjective activity in which it originates. Against this attitude—whose most prominent representatives for Fichte are Spinoza and Schelling—, the *Science of Knowledge* invariably brings out the same demand: we need to "defetishize," to take back into account, the activity that was forgotten in favor of the intellectual product that the dogmatic system is, i.e., in the final analysis, to reflect its own reflection or think what we are saying:

> The *Science of Knowledge* argued . . . that in dealing with these products of the fixed form of reflection, they (the dogmatics) could at least meditate on themselves and think what was thought. Realizing, however, that if they accepted this proposition, their cherished illusion would vanish and what they take for the thing-in-itself would clearly prove to be just a simple thought, they hold that they ought never be forced to reflect on this point. . . . In this, they utterly fail to see that, quite independently of the fact that they are reflecting or not on their act of thinking, this act remains in itself as it is and necessarily keeps the figure given it by the form of the limitation in which they accomplish it. . . . Their absolute, of which they can think nothing save that it exists, thus remains something objective in this case—projected by vision and opposed in itself, in essence, to this objective thing. . . ."[15]

So we see, though "fetishism" is not mentioned, the thing is described here, even in terms that prove perfectly adequate, since Fichte is using the concept of projection to designate the process of metaphysical objectification. It is also noteworthy that fetishism is biased and tendentious, just as the critique of it is biased and tendentious: it aims at a theoretical actualization of the requirement of autonomy and freedom that was destroyed by dogmatic "obscurity."

—Thus, the critique of dogmatism is also a reparation, if metaphysical discourse—although, or rather because, it is perfectly conceptually coherent—eliminates, as such, the conditions of finitude, thus of its own appropriation by the finite subject. But no mistake about it, despite appearances, the formula is not at all paradoxical, and Fichte's critique of metaphysics in no way promises a certain mode that sees "violence" and "repression" in any rational discourse. On the contrary, Fichte merely revives if not the letter, at least the spirit of the "Transcendental Dialectic" in which Kant clearly showed how the absolute extension of the concept characteristic of metaphysics (the transition from the categories to the Ideas) must necessarily result in the elimination of the condition that in the "Transcendental Aesthetic" guaranteed the autonomy of the sphere of finitude (the nonidentity of the conceptual and the real). So, to defetishize is to recall man to his limits, i.e., to himself, and thus to make up for the wrong he suffered in what we may call reification. This critical activity is not effected through any "sentimentalism"; we are not contrasting "intuition" with "concept," as in a *Lebensphilosophie,*[16] no more than we are restoring some primitive reality once concealed by reification. The very structure of the *Science of Knowledge* precludes this reading: first, as we have seen, dialectics does not originate in any positivity but starts in pure illusion to extract its truth, and the resulting "reparation" does not have the sense of a restoration. On the other hand, the critique of metaphysics, far from presupposing some renunciation of the modern philosophical project of intelligibility, is done in the name of additional awareness, in contrast to a metaphysics that does not totally rationalize its discourse because, to achieve the desired logical coherence, it must avoid problematizing the place from which the discourse is uttered.[17] This way, conversely to what goes on in dogmatic metaphysics, finitude is here conceived through additional awareness: if the extension of the concept to the Absolute (to the assertion of the identity of the real and the rational characteristic of all metaphysical discourse) gets away from finitude, the realization of the preconditions of metaphysics leads there, so that Fichte's critique is neither irrational nor romantic (aiming to restore something that existed before it was eclipsed). It is interesting here to compare Fichte's and Heidegger's deconstructions of metaphysics: both of them—along with Kant, moreover—lead to the positing of finitude, the "ontological difference," and mark as such increased awareness in relation to the somehow naive belief in the identity of the real and the rational. Given his critique of "subjectivity," however, Heidegger can only deny this increase in awareness, so that his critique of metaphysics must necessarily include a "romantic" step, as Adorno's criticism shows, whatever its limitations in other respects.[18] It is also in this sense that the thought of the young Fichte is entirely opposed to any Restoration.

—Fichte's critique of metaphysics must thus inevitably become "political," at least in the sense in which it attacks the biased and tendentious discourse of dogmatism and thus attempts to restore man to himself by establishing an area of intersubjectivity or communication. Connecting the question of intersubjectivity with that of the critique of metaphysics, Fichte got his basic inspiration from the *Critique of Judgment*. To be convinced of this, all we need do is recall the close connection between the "Transcendental Dialectic" and the theory of direct communication[19] (intersubjectivity) elaborated in connection with the judgment of taste in the third *Critique:* what enables aesthetic judgment to function is precisely the "residue" that Kant, after the critique of special metaphysics, calls (in the appendix to the "Transcendental Dialectic") the "regulative usage" of the Ideas of reason, and (in the introduction to the *Critique of Judgment*) the "principle of reflection." Once deconstructed, the metaphysical, i.e., defetishized, Ideas preserve a *sense,* a schematic (symbolic) function: it is uniquely in relation to our regulative requirement of systematicity (thus in relation to the regulative use of the theological Idea) that the beautiful as the contingent agreement of the sensibility and the understanding, as the "legality of the contingent," is possible, for it is basically only a "trace" of the metaphysical Ideas, or, more exactly, of the exigency that they continue to manifest after this deconstruction.[20]

Thus, already in Kant, the critique of metaphysics is the direct opening of an intersubjective area, that of aesthetics. Fichte's originality, in contrast to Kant's, was to transpose the question of intersubjectivity from the domain of aesthetics to that of rights and politics, as Philonenko was the first Fichte scholar to note:

> [I]n Fichte's philosophy, the fundamental stage in the problematic of intersubjectivity is not aesthetics—it is the philosophy of rights. At the beginning of his book on natural right Fichte describes the constitutive relation of intersubjectivity. Most of the problems that aesthetics gives rise to are found in the philosophy of rights. Thus we see the

problem of communication, of meaning, appear just as the concepts of individuality and community are essential. Are rights thinkable without intersubjectivity? What's more, aren't rights and beauty essentially human creations, and isn't the theory of rights located at the same level as aesthetics?[21]

In the next chapter we shall see in greater detail how in the first chapter of the *Science of Rights* Fichte bases his deduction of intersubjectivity on this critique of metaphysics. We can already see, however, in what sense the critique of dogmatic metaphysics can open onto the problematic of communication; what Kant saw as an aesthetic problem becomes for Fichte a legal and political problem. This is, moreover, a theme that appeared in embryo in Fichte's first political writings where, in 1793, the opposition between the monarchy and the republic was presented as an antinomy that in many respects foreshadowed the structure of the *Science of Knowledge*. As Philonenko has shown, in the *Beiträge* "every state—i.e., every association, monarchical or otherwise—presupposes a basic social relation, defined by the core meaning of the term *Gesellschaft*. This primordial social relation is a state of peace. . . . We call it *thesis*. As the self that corresponds to the first principle of the *Science of Knowledge*, this state of peace appears against the background of this primordial social relation. It is clear that monarchies represent something in opposition to the primordial social relation. In this sense the monarchical state corresponds to the not-self, and we may consider it as the *antithesis*. Hence the conflict between thesis and antithesis."[22]

A brief comparison of Fichte's project with that of the Critical Theory of the Frankfurt School may yield a firmer grasp of the fruitfulness of the articulation thus put in place between the critique of metaphysics and the critique of politics. Because the difference between the two projects is clearly too important to be analyzed in the present book, I shall merely note how Critical Theory repeats, consciously or not,[23] certain essential theses of the critique of illusion in the *Science of Knowledge*.

Faced with metaphysics, Critical Theory's taking on the project of defetishization shows up in the famous distinction between traditional theory and critical theory, a distinction whereby Critical Theory aims to expose the human and objective self-interests operating behind Critical Theory's boastful shows objectivity and impartiality. For Horkheimer, traditional theory is indeed characterized by fetishism, for it proves unable to reflect on itself, to take charge of its own history, and to determine its own direction: "In traditional theoretical thinking, the genesis of particular objective facts, the practical application of the conceptual systems by which it grasps the facts, and the role of such systems in action, are all taken to be external to the theoretical thinking itself";[24] in this science is positivistic and hence fetishistic, for it isolates its activity from human work and, as such, falsely presents itself as purely objective:

> Science itself does not know "why it orders facts in just this direction, nor why it concentrates on some objects and not others. What science is lacking is reflection about itself, a knowledge of the social motives that impel it in a certain direction, to a concern with the moon, for example, and not with human well-being. To be true, science would have to act critically with regard to itself and what produced it.[25]

It would be only too easy to produce many quotations in which scientific objectivity is attacked as falsely neutral[26] and critical theory declared the weapon that gives rise, under the deceptive appearance of positivist impartiality, to the role of subjectivity (self-interests), critical theory differing from traditional theory precisely in that the former assumes, as it were, its proper subjectivity since "there is . . . no theory of society . . . that does not contain political motivations, and the truth of these must be decided not in supposedly neutral reflection"[27]—in rooting its critique in a universal self-interest.[28] No doubt Horkheimer's *Critical Theory* has terms of reference that are different from Fichte's dialectics: the criticism is of an historically produced ideology more than an a priori metaphysical illusion, and the criticism itself relies more on Marxism (as the preface of the famous manifesto indicates) than on transcendental philosophy. For all this, however, the *structural* analogy with Fichte's philosophy is remarkable in this initial period during which Critical Theory was still heavily influenced by a Marxist conception of ideology.

It is otherwise undeniable that Critical Theory, particularly starting in the 1940s, underwent considerable modification. Without going into detail,[29] we may note the fact that its evolution was marked by a corresponding change in the Frankfurt thinkers' notions of enlightenment and ideology. In brief, the concept of the Enlightenment was increasingly used to designate not simply a historically and materially locatable moment but the very structure of all thought, which, as Martin Jay noted, necessarily implies having recourse to critical concepts other than those of Marxism:

In fact, the notion of the Enlightenment underwent a basic change in the forties. Instead of being the cultural correlate of the ascending bourgeoisie, it was expanded to include the entire spectrum of Western thought. . . . In *Eclipse of Reason* [Horkheimer] went so far as to say that "this mentality of man as the master [which was the essence of the Enlightenment view] can be traced back to the first chapters of *Genesis.*" Thus, although Horkheimer and Adorno still used language reminiscent of Marxism . . . they no longer sought answers to cultural questions in the material substructure of society.[30]

Ideology, particularly in Adorno's thought, thus merges with the metaphysics of culturally realized identity (which he calls "the administered world,"[31] a realization whose practical effect is the elimination of the finite subject, the "liquidation of the particular."

I shall not elaborate on this familiar theme here, but merely stress how, in his *Negative Dialectics,* Adorno conceives of the process of the finite subject's liquidation: with the appearance of Cartesian subjectivity—thus with the appearance of constitutive subjectivity, which in Kant was to become 'transcendental"—everything happens as though the subject had to posit himself as "active and victorious," "master and owner of nature," according to the Cartesian formula. Dialectically, however, this initially liberating domination of nature is transformed into something else in a movement that, according to Adorno, occurs in the history of philosophy in the transition from Kant to Hegel: though Kant still rightly maintains "the duality of subject and object . . . against the thought's inherent claim to total" (*ND,* 175), it is by a kind of (almost incoherent) resistance to the inevitable consequences implied by the transcendental subject's positing; so that his "more consistent"[32] idealist successors will merely have to work out the implications to achieve the finite subject's total liquidation which coincides with the victory of the absolute subject: "The universal domination of mankind by the exchange value—a domination which a priori keeps the subjects from being subjects and degrades subjectivity itself to a mere object—makes an untruth of the general principle that claims to establish the subject's predominance. The surplus of the transcendental subject is the deficit of the utterly reduced empirical subject" (*ND,* 178).

This is how we need to understand one of the major theses in *Negative Dialectics,* which is that the supreme triumph of philosophy (the Hegelian system) is at the same time its cruelest failure:[33] when the transcendental subject reaches its maximum—i.e., for Adorno, when it becomes the Hegelian Absolute subject—the empirical subject is totally reified: "The constitutive subject of philosophy is more of a thing than the specific psychological content which is excreted, as naturalistic and reified. The more autocratically the I [self] rises above entity, the greater its imperceptible objectification and ironic retraction of its constitutive role" (*ND*, 176–77). Thus, this analysis of metaphysics perfectly converges—structurally, at least—with the one we saw set up at the beginning of the *Science of Knowledge*. From then on, it is not at all surprising that, in Adorno also, the philosophical aim—here, it is unimportant whether it fails or not—tends to right the wrong done to the particular individual in metaphysical ideology and, a fortiori, obviously, in this realization of Hegelianism that the administered world is for him. And, as in Fichte, this critique of illusion is claimed not to entail the least "romanticism,"[34] meaning it is done neither in the name of sentiment against the concept, nor with a view to some return to a lost authenticity—because, as in Fichte again, awareness proves capable of grasping its own illusion: "The power of awareness goes far enough to grasp its own illusion. We can rationally recognize how unbridled rationality, escaping itself, turns false and truly mythological. The *ratio* turns into irrationality as, *in its necessary progression,* it ignores the fact that the disappearance of its substrate, as weakened as it is, is its own doing."

In other words, the subject may perceive its illusion, but the illusion is still necessary, and the result is the reification of the subject: three theses that Fichte would doubtless have accepted. Under these conditions, the task of *Negative Dialectics* must be allied to that of the *Science of Knowledge:* by deconstructing the metaphysical illusion of totality—an illusion that here again becomes manifest in the philosophy of history—we need to preserve the possibility of the Other by relying on the lone critical resistance, which is purely negative, of the subject that was eliminated: "Against [the ideology that ... deduces dominion either from such allegedly inalienable forms of social organization as centralization ... or from forms of consciousness abstracted out of the real process—the ratio] there remains the vigorous critique of a politics fetishized into being-in-itself, or of a spirit bloated in its particularity" (*ND*, 323). And, again as in Fichte, the roots of ideology are formed in the metaphysics of history by the theory of the cunning of reason:

Touched upon by events of the twentieth century, however, is the idea of historic totality as a calculable economic necessity.[35] Only if things

100

> might have gone differently: if the totality is recognized as a socially necessary semblance, as the hypostasis of the universal pressed out of individual human beings; if its claim to be absolute is broken—only then will a critical social consciousness retain its freedom to think that things might be different some day. Theory cannot shift the huge weight of historic necessity unless the necessity has been recognized as realized appearance and historic determination is known as a metaphysical accident. Such cognition is frustrated by the metaphysics of history. (*ND*, 323)

To wit, the metaphysical illusion of totality was, as it were, achieved (the totalitarian phenomenon characteristic of the twentieth century), and the denunciation of this illusion (a defetishization of politics) is thwarted by the metaphysics of history, i.e., among others, by the theories of the cunning of reason that postulate the identity of the rational and the real. Here again, there is nothing inconsistent with the dialectics of the *Science of Knowledge* (even though, unfortunately keeping the strictly mythical idea of a materialist genesis of illusion, Adorno again declares it "socially" necessary).[36]

We still need to see how Fichte, starting with transcendental philosophy and not from historical materialism, manages to articulate his political thought in the deconstruction of metaphysics whose premises we have just indicated.

The Deduction of Rights as an Area of Intersubjectivity

1—From Objectivity to Intersubjectivity

Without making a detailed study of this deduction, we may note with Georges Gurvitch that its interest and originality lie in its synthesis of "individualistic" and "universalistic" ideas of rights; although, as Gurvitch shows,[1] the aporias of legal individualism (whose model he takes to be Rousseau and especially the thought of Kantian jurists) inevitably result in the absolute separation of the domains of rights and of ethics, legal universalism (the most cogent version of which is Hegel's philosophy of rights) implies a reduction of the moral to the legal. In his deduction of intersubjectivity Fichte meant to resolve this antinomy in a synthesis which Gurvitch—seeing in Fichte the great herald of the idea of social rights—said was "the most thorough and successful ever known in the history of moral ideas."[2]

Fichte concluded that any attempt to deduce rights from ethics was aporetic because, far from being deducible from the idea of an individual moral duty, the concept of rights presupposes intersubjectivity. Thus, rights must be distinguished not only from ethics but also from politics.[3] Given this distinction, however, the philosophy of rights proves to be genuine political philosophy: indeed, if the philosophy of rights treats, according to a formula that Strauss would have accepted, "the questions that can be raised concerning the particular determination of the one and only just constitution," politics in Fichte's sense is the application of the pure principles of the science of rights to historical facticity by means of the state.

As Gurvitch realized,[4] Fichte's distinction between the legal and the political is connected with the idea of the gap between society and the state, the state being always a means (and never an end in itself) for actualizing rights within the higher reality of society. Contrasting with both ethics and politics in an anti-individualistic and antistatist idea, rights are nevertheless articulated with these other two spheres. In a formulation that probably somewhat caricatures but does not, I believe, essentially distort Fichte's thought, we could interpret the articulation this way: the domain of rights (of society) is located between the ethical domain of the individual and the political domain of the state, the state being a means for actualizing rights, which are the preconditions of ethics.

For Fichte, rights cannot be deduced from ethical individualism because at the level on which rights are located (i.e., by definition, before the actualization of the moral ideal), the notion of individuality implies that of intersubjectivity, as the first chapter of the *Science of Rights* undertakes to show:

> Man becomes man only among men; and since he can only be human, and would not exist at all without being human, it follows that *if man is to exist at all, there must be men.* This supposition is not arbitrary, nor is it an opinion based on past experience or other probabilistic considerations, but a truth strictly deduced from the conception of man. As soon as you proceed to determine this conception fully, you are driven from thinking of a single man to the assumption of another one by means of which to explain the first. Hence, the conception of man is not the conception of a single one, for such a one is unthinkable, but of a breed. (*SR,* 60–61; translation modified)

At the start of the *Science of Rights,* Fichte states his project: to come up with a nonempirical, noninductive solution to the problem of the existence of others. This problem must be solved prior to thinking about rights since "rights can be spoken of only on the condition that a person is conceived *as* a person, that is, as an individual or, in other words, as having a relation to other individuals, and that between him and them a society if not real, then at least possible can be imagined" (*SR,* 159).[5] Fichte is thus criticizing all previous philosophies, particularly those dealing with rights, for not first showing the need for intersubjectivity or, which comes to the same thing, the impossibility of thinking of the individual as isolated. This criticism even applies to Kant's *Critique of Pure Reason,* as Fichte clearly hints in his "Lectures on the Vocation of the Scholar."

In the second lecture, Fichte poses the problem in these terms: "The concept of society presupposes that there actually are rational beings apart from oneself. It also presupposes the existence of some characteristic features that enable us to distinguish these beings from all nonrational creatures. . . . How do we arrive at this presupposition, and what are the characteristic features of rational beings?"[6]

Fichte rejects a simple appeal to experience as "superficial and un-satisfying,"[7] for experience as the "system of our representations" does not rigorously prove the existence of other rational beings gen-uinely external to us: "All that experience teaches us is that our con-sciousness contains *the representation* of rational beings outside of ourselves."[8] The question of the existence of others thus appears as one aspect—and, as we shall see, the most important one—of the problem of the critique of idealism understood as the reduction of existence to the representation of a subject that is closed in on itself. Now, on this point, Kant's answer is merely empirical, for it sees the distinguishing sign of humanity in the goal (the intentional action).[9] The problem is then clear: the goal that, assuredly, is the necessary condition for the manifestation of freedom, that of man's essence, is not, however, a sufficient condition, for there exist beings that are simply natural, but still finalized: organized beings. Hence Fichte's critique:

> The first, though merely negative, distinguishing characteristic of ra-tionality, or at least the first one to come to mind, is efficacy governed by concept, i.e., purposeful activity. What bears the distinguishing fea-tures of purposefulness may have a rational author, whereas that to which the concept of purposefulness is entirely inapplicable surely has no rational author. Yet this feature is ambiguous. The distinguish-ing characteristic of purposefulness is the harmony of multiplicity in a unity. But many types of such harmony are explicable merely by natu-ral laws—not *mechanical* laws, but *organic* ones certainly. In order, therefore, to be able to infer convincingly from a particular experi-ence to its rational cause we require some feature in addition [to pur-posefulness]. Even in those cases where it operates purposefully, na-ture operates in accordance with *necessary laws.* Reason always operates *freely.*.... The only question is how one can tell the differ-ence between an effect one has experienced which occurs necessarily and one which occurs freely.[10]

Fichte's question helps us see the decisive importance, for criti-cal philosophy, of the problem of intersubjectivity: we have seen that Fichte saw the deduction of the existence of others as an indispens-able prior condition for any thinking about rights; we have also seen that, once this deduction is made, it should allow us to "refute ideal-ism" and hence to solve the critical problem of representation. Thus, Fichte recalls, at the start of the "Second Lecture on the Vocation of the Scholar," that his purpose is to "refute" the "egoists"[11] (the ideal-ists); a prerequisite for a doctrine of rights and a refutation of idealism, the deduction of intersubjectivity—the proof of the existence of others—finally addresses the central difficulty created by Kant's solution to the third antinomy, i.e., the conflict between freedom and determinism.

This solution rests, as we know, on the distinction between the sensory (phenomenal) world and the intelligible (noumenal) world, with the deterministic rule of causality holding for the former, and freedom being possible in the latter. Fichte found this solution unsatisfactory: human actions are—at least when observed from the outside—simple phenomena, and the question obviously arises of knowing what, at the phenomenal level, distinguishes a free action (the effect of a reasonable being) from a determined action (the effect of natural law). This is the real stake in Fichte's critique of finality as a purely empirical criterion of the recognition of the existence of others, an inadequate criterion because it does not fully enable us (owing mainly to the existence of "natural ends") to distinguish between "an effect of freedom" and "an effect of necessity," as the first chapter of the *Science of Rights* reminds us: "What effects can be explained only as the effects of a rational cause? The answer 'the effects that must necessarily be preceded by a conception of them' is true, but not sufficient, for the higher and more difficult question remains 'What, then, effects must we say were possible only after a prior conception of them?" (*SR*, 57–58). Fichte solves this problem in the second chapter of the *Science of Rights* by an admirable phenomenology of the body whose significance I have discussed elsewhere.[12]

The philosophical significance of the stakes of this deduction of intersubjectivity, thus specified in its three aspects, becomes clear when we observe Fichte's method: starting with an inquiry into the preconditions for self-awareness, the method involves going back to the necessity for positing the existence of others so that intersubjectivity appears as a precondition for individual subjectivity itself: "The concept of individuality is . . . reciprocal, i.e., a concept we can have only in relation to another thinking, its form being conditioned by this other thinking, and, moreover, by the *same* thinking of it. This concept is possible in every rational being only when it is posited as completed through another individual. Hence the concept of individuality never belongs to me alone, but through my own admission and the admission of the other individual, it is both *mine* and *his* and *his* and *mine;* a common concept in which two awarenesses are united into one" (*SR*, 72).

Intersubjectivity thus appears a necessary condition for the very existence of individuality and self-awareness. Now, because intersub-jectivity is by definition a relation between free beings, this relation may take a legal form. Hence Fichte's initially rather surprising con-clusion that in the final analysis "a precondition of self-awareness is . . . the conception of law (of rights)" (*SR,* 79). In this deduction, as Fichte is always reminding us, the step that leads to the positing of individuality as the precondition for self-awareness, and then inter-subjectivity and rights as preconditions for individuality, is a strictly *theoretical* step, the domain of rights being not only distinct from that of morality but even opposed to it.[13] In this sense, and even be-fore we examine Fichte's argument, we can see that the deduction of intersubjectivity takes place at the level of a refutation of idealism, so that §4 of the *Science of Rights* concludes, "The question concerning the ground of the reality of objects is now answered. The reality of the world—of course for us, i.e., for all finite reason—is a precondi-tion for self-awareness; for we cannot posit ourselves without posit-ing something outside ourselves to which we must ascribe the same reality that we ascribe to ourselves" (*SR,* 62).

Thus, at this exact point, we have a first clear view of the criticism of metaphysics made in terms of a philosophy of freedom or the fu-ture, and there then appears the determination of this future as a legal and political space of intersubjectivity. This articulation may be expressed in two ways, negatively and positively:

- Negatively: a metaphysics that asserts the identity of being and thinking makes possible and even necessary a philosophy of his-tory that, politically, results in a shift to historicism.
- Positively: a critique of this metaphysics (by asserting the exis-tence of the world and of others as the preconditions for self-awareness) makes possible a philosophy of history in which man is thought of as free, and the future as undetermined for all eternity.[14]

The change from a critique of metaphysics to a philosophy of history as the effect of freedom is already built into the structure of the *Science of Knowledge* which, by destroying the metaphysical il-lusion of the absolute self—a theoretical illusion of a substrate ante-rior to the appearance of the world, temporality, and intersubjectiv-ity—, makes this absolute self into a simple practical idea that merely defines a future. These two points are spelled out in the deduction of intersubjectivity. Rights thus appear as both the solution to the problem of the refutation of idealism (hence as the final step in

Fichte's deconstruction of metaphysics) and the goal of the philosophy of history as a philosophy of freedom.

To determine the meaning and scope of this articulation, and to see how rights as the theoretical precondition for self-awareness complete the refutation of idealism (the deconstruction of metaphysics) in Fichte's *Science of Knowledge,* we need to sketch his solution to the antinomy of realism and idealism.

We have already seen how the dogmatic versions of idealism and realism have failed; idealism tries to deduce the object from self-awareness by reducing the passivity of representation (the "illusion" of a not-self) to a difference between absolute and least quanta of activity; the problem with idealism is the utter inexplicability of object-awareness, i.e., the reason why the finite subject refers this difference between two quanta to a term outside itself. Realism faces the reverse problem: explaining self-awareness on the basis of object-awareness by the hypothesis of the thing in itself's causal action on the self, it cannot use the theory of "reflection" to explain what is then necessarily its own self-awareness.

The solution to the problem—representation—must therefore consist in a synthesis of idealism and realism that fully explains the indissoluble connection between the self-awareness and the awareness of the world. In his *Science of Knowledge* Fichte called this the "synthesis of determinability." I shall make no attempt here to give a detailed analysis of this synthesis, which probably represents the most difficult and obscure passage, not just in the *Science of Knowledge,* but possibly in the whole history of philosophy.[15] We will merely examine the step in which, after introducing the notion of "independent activity" (to be defined shortly), Fichte for the first time transcends the dialectics of realism and idealism in favor of the correct solution to the problem of representation.[16] We will then see how this solution necessarily brings into play the notion of intersubjectivity, which the *Science of Rights* will specify more fully (and, above all, more concretely). Then, and only then, the desired articulation between the two steps of the young Fichte's political thought—his critique of metaphysics and his philosophy of rights— will be brought clearly to light, for we will see the precise manner in which the idea of an intersubjective political space is possible only in and through a critique of the metaphysics of history that reduces the future to the past; furthermore, we will see the indissoluble and reciprocal link between the critique of metaphysics and the political idea if the doctrine of rights is indeed conceivable only after the destruction of metaphysical illusion and if, conversely, the destruction of metaphysics leads to the question of representation (the problem of the refutation of idealism) in such terms that its solution can only be some idea of intersubjectivity.

The three propositions that, from the introduction of the notion of "independent activity," lead to the first correct (critical) solution of the problem posed by the antinomy of idealism and realism are as follows (I indicate them primarily as what is to be understood):

> (1) An independent activity is determined by the relation between activity and passivity.
> (2) A relation between activity and passivity is determined by an independent activity.
> (3) Each is determined by the other, and it matters not whether we go from the relation between activity and passivity to independent activity, or vice versa. (*SK*, 143)

It must be admitted that Fichte's language here is almost unremittingly hermetic. Nevertheless, thanks to Philonenko's interpretation, we can indicate the general meaning of these three propositions clearly enough to trace the thread of the argument without going into all its technicalities.

We will thus make the following comments about these three propositions:

1) The "relation between activity and passivity" denotes experience (representation), i.e., the reciprocity between (active) self-awareness and (passive) object-awareness. The fact that this reciprocity determines an "independent activity" simply means that the philosopher uses the fact of representation or, if you will, the common awareness, to produce a genuine explanation of it by discovering its cause. The cause is an "independent activity," for it is external to the reciprocity thus explained (for the dogmatic realist, this will be "substance," for the dogmatic idealist "imagination," as we will see in the following).

2) The second proposition is a bit more complex: it assumes some thinking about the way Fichte explained (according to the first proposition) the experience of the common awareness: it is indeed the philosopher who has just indicated the cause of this experience, and for him this "indicate" is an activity that is also independent of the reciprocity we are examining. So we will say that the first independent activity (the real cause of the experience) is "material,"

while the second activity (the thinking by which the philosopher posits this cause) is "formal."

3) There is no essential difference, however, between the philosopher and the common awareness; the philosopher is also a self-awareness reflecting about the object-awareness he is seeking to understand (in this case, the common awareness); his awareness thus has the same structure as that of the common awareness, even though his philosophical activity is not that of this awareness. Hence, three problems in which the third will decompose itself:

a) First, one must "synthesize," i.e., make the two independent activities compatible: in plain language—and this is the essence of the criticism—the real explanation of experience should not contradict the philosophical thought positing this explanation (as we shall shortly see, dogmatic idealism and dogmatic realism never manage to solve this problem).

b) Next, one must bring about the synthesis of the form and content of the common awareness itself as the relation (which is equivalent to form which is equivalent to sequence) of activity to passivity (which is equivalent to matter which is equivalent to limits).

c) Finally, one must synthesize the first two syntheses, i.e., the synthesis of philosophy (as a synthesis of the explanation of experience and reflection about experience) and of the common awareness as a synthesis of the reciprocity between its active or passive terms.

At this point (c) (the third step of the third proposition), we finally reach the correct (critical) philosophical point of view: we will then be in a position to solve the problem of representation and to make every step in this solution explicit.

We must now examine the elements in this extremely complex argument so that we can understand the transition from the critique of metaphysics (of realism and idealism) to the philosophy of rights.

We shall set aside the "methodical" way in which the independent activity is posited and interest ourselves directly in the meaning it assumes in the "illusory" solution to the problem of representation offered by dogmatic realism and dogmatic idealism.[17] So the first proposition to consider is that "the relation between activity and passivity determines an independent activity." Here we need to understand how "the reciprocity"—i.e., the reciprocity between awareness and its object—must be explained, and thus to determine its real foundation.

The first explanation to suggest itself is that of realism, which relies on the principle of causality. We have seen how realism went from the self's passivity (of the affection) to the not-self's activity on the self (of a thing in itself). We may say that in this sense the self's passivity is "the ideal reason" (*Ideal-Grund*) for the not-self's activity (*SK,* 145). We obtain this reasoning by applying the category of reciprocal determination: to the self's passivity must correspond some activity in the not-self.

But a new question immediately arises which clearly shows the need to introduce the notion of independent activity: no doubt the self's passivity makes it necessary to posit activity in the not-self, but how can we explain this passivity? Explaining the self's passivity by the not-self's activity lands us in a circle. "Once passivity has been posited in the self, it will be granted without hesitation that activity is posited in the not-self; but why then, in general, is activity posited? The answer to this question is no longer to be found in the principle of interdetermination, but in the higher grounding principle" (*SK,* 145). In other words, there should now be indicated a real (not just ideal) foundation of the reciprocal relation between act and passivity, and, being real, this foundation must necessarily be independent of the reciprocity.

Thus we will distinguish two activities in the not-self: the not-self's activity in the reciprocal relation that is dependent activity, for it is posited thanks to the category of reciprocal determination based on the self's passivity; and "an activity of the not-self independent of the reciprocity and already presupposed in the possibility thereof" that will be posited as "the real ground of passivity" (*SK,* 146). We then understand the sense of the first proposition from the viewpoint of dogmatic realism. It is stated as follows: "Through the interplay between passivity of the self and activity of the not-self, an independent activity of the latter was *posited;* through the very same interplay, it is also *determined;* it is posited to provide the ground for a passivity posited in the self" (*SK,* 148).[18]

Now let us see what meaning the first proposition has in idealism, according to the category of substantiality. As we saw in the preceding chapter, the difficulty inherent in the viewpoint of substantiality is that the idealist explanation of the not-self (reducing it to a least quantum of activity) means that passivity and activity are not qualitatively different (as in realism), but merely quantitatively different:[19]

"How is a restricted activity of the self to be distinguished from a restricted activity of the not-self? Which means nothing less than: How, under these conditions, are the self and the not-self to be still distinguished at all? For the ground of distinction between self and not-self, whereby the first was supposed to be active and the second passive, has been abolished" (*SK*, 149). So it appears impossible to determine an activity independent of the relation between activity and passivity, for the good and simple reason that since passivity is a restricted activity, it becomes impossible to distinguish between the self's limited activity and the not-self's limited activity, both of them coinciding in the simply quantitative concept of passivity. The solution consists in positing that the self's limited activity has a specific character that absolutely distinguishes it from the not-self, i.e., its spontaneity: "This property of the self, however, which cannot possibly be attributed to the not-self, is *to posit and be posited absolutely, without any ground* (§1)" (*SK*, 149). Thus, the distinguishing feature of this restricted activity of the not-self's activity is its absolute freedom, its being stripped of a ground, though limited if it occurs (hence distinct from the absolute activity that is referred to an object). Therefore, it is this restricted activity—as distinct from not-self's activity (which always has a ground) and from an absolute activity (which is not restricted)—that is the independent activity. Fichte saw this restricted activity "from two points of view" (*SK*, 150); when seen as located in the reciprocity, it is dependent, limited, and hence passive; but when seen as spontaneous activity, it is independent, for, as we have seen, it is distinct from absolute (total) activity as well as from the not-self's activity. Fichte saw this independent activity as "the imagination" which thus appears as the Leibnizian analog of "Spinozistic *natura naturans*."[20]

Thus, these are the two dogmatic explanations posited to solve the problem of representation (the problem of the reciprocity between awareness and its object). To get beyond these illusory and antinomial explanations, we need to make a remark whose methodical importance cannot be overstated: these two explanations of object-awareness were themselves posited by the (philosopher's) awareness of objects (the object here being the other object-awareness, i.e., the common awareness). The whole question thus is how the explanations provided (by positing an independent activity) of the proper relation of the awareness observed by the philosopher, are also valid for the philosopher's awareness itself. In short, it must be that the philosopher reflects on his own reflection.[21]

This is the stake of the analysis of the second proposition ("a relation between activity and passivity is determined by an independent activity") in which the term of independent activity is now understood in its formal sense; from the material point of view of the reciprocity (i.e., in terms of the act-passivity relation), the independent activity was, as we have seen, what we must posit to make sense of the terms (Spinoza's *natura naturans,* Leibniz's "Imagination"). On the other hand, from the "formal" point of view, i.e., from the putting into relation or connection of the terms, the independent activity is thus merely of the philosopher's reflection which provides the material explanation of the relation (of the common awareness).

As Philonenko remarks, in this role intersubjectivity appears as an "essential step in the resolution of the problem of objectivity" since "to prove how an awareness may be of a self and of an object amounts to establishing a relation between two awarenesses."[22] And, conversely, we shall see how the nonresolution of the problem of objectivity in dogmatic realism and dogmatic idealism results precisely from the fact that philosophical reflection is not itself reflected, so that the solution to the problem of representation provided by the material independent activity is incompatible with the philosopher's reflection (the formal independent activity): the explanation provided by philosophical awareness denies philosophical awareness as such. Thus, by deconstructing the dogmatics' error in their method, we see how the question of objectivity can only be resolved through an adequate idea of intersubjectivity. At this point we have indicated how the doctrine of rights, as a doctrine of intersubjectivity, may appear the concrete solution to what seems to be the merely theoretical problem of the preconditions of awareness.

From the viewpoint of realism, therefore, the formal independent activity may be defined as "a *positing by means of a nonpositing* (a conferring in consequence of a deprivation), or a transference" (*SK,* 152). It is from the nonpositing of the self's activity that we posit activity in the not-self. The problem with the realist view once again involves the philosophizing self actively[23] positing the observed self (that which is object-awareness, as a term of the reciprocity) as passive. We shall come back to this point. Conversely, from the viewpoint of idealism, the formal independent activity is defined as a "nonpositing by a positing" (*SK,* 153), because it is on the basis of the total activity that a restricted activity (passivity, the nonposited) is posited: "In the interplay of *substantiality,* activity is to be posited as limited by means of absolute totality; that is, the portion of absolute totality that is excluded by the limit is posited as *not* posited in the positing of the limited activity, as missing therefrom. Thus the purely formal character of this reciprocity is a *nonpositing* by way of a positing" (*SK,* 67). Further on, we shall see how the problem of the idealist positing is the converse of that of realism.

First, we should indicate how the first two positings are composed in the third, such that "each [of the two first propositions] is determined by the other," so that "it matters not whether we go from a relation between activity and passivity to independent activity, or vice versa" (*SK,* 143; translation modified). This proposition immediately presupposes three others when we apply the difference between the form and the matter of the reciprocity; we need to compose synthetically (1) the formal independent activity and the material independent activity, (2) the form and the matter of the reciprocity, and (3) the reciprocity as a synthetic unity of form and matter.[24] Then and only then, with the antinomial oppositions composed, we can grasp the solution to the problem of representation and see how closely it depends on the notion of intersubjectivity. It is also along this path that, conversely, we will understand how the errors of the realist and the idealist lie in an empiricism of reflection, an inability to reflect on their own reflection, so that the formal independent activity and the material independent activity are compatible.

To avoid needlessly weighing down this analysis—whose purpose is simply to show the connection between the problem of objectivity (of representation) as set out in the *Science of Knowledge,* and the idea of legal intersubjectivity elaborated in the *Science of Rights*—I will confine myself, instead of following Fichte's text in detail,[25] to studying the three following points:

1) first, the errors of dogmatic metaphysics and its inability to compose the duality of the independent activity, and for that very reason to resolve the two other syntheses;
2) Fichte's solution to this question, one that also solves the problem of representation;
3) the connection between intersubjectivity and objectivity presupposed by this solution and the transition from the *Science of Knowledge* to the theory of rights.[26]

1. Fichte examines the first point in E. III α. Using the term "transition" for the formal independent activity (i.e., philosophical reflec-

tion about the observed reciprocity between awareness and its object) and the letter X for the material independent activity (the ground of the reciprocity), Fichte defines the error of idealism and dogmatism as follows: "That the first [formal independent] activity should determine the second [material independent activity] would mean that the transition itself is the ground of that to which transition is made; by the mere transition, the transit becomes possible (an idealist claim). That the second activity should determine the first would mean that the transition, as an action, is grounded on that to which transition is made; insofar as the latter is posited, the transition itself is immediately posited (a dogmatic claim)" (SK, 156).

Thus we see that both realism and idealism make the same mistake of suppressing the duality of the independent activity by reducing one of its aspects to the other:

Realism resides—not surprisingly—in the negation of the formal independent activity (philosophical reflection or self-awareness) in favor of material independent activity (the ground of experience): philosophical reflection on experience (self-awareness) has exactly the same explanation as object-awareness which is one term of the reciprocity. Both terms are produced by the material independent activity: "That to which transition is made (the relation of awareness to its object) ground the transition as an action" (i.e., fully explains how philosophical reflection puts awareness in a reciprocal relation with its object). Now we should recall that this explanation is impossible, for it takes no account of self-awareness: the analysis of the antinomy made clear that in realism philosophical awareness in fact surreptitiously played the role of self-awareness of the mode (of the observed object-awareness), and that this was necessary for passivity to be perceived as such (necessary because the material independent activity is posited from passivity). If, therefore, philosophical awareness is explained as object-awareness, self-awareness becomes incomprehensible, and the causal reasoning in which we go from the self's passivity to the not-self's activity collapses.

Idealism makes the converse error: it posits that the transition (philosophical reflection, which is identical to the formal independent activity) makes possible reciprocity ("the ground of that to which transition is made"). Once again, therefore, the duality of the independent activity is not composed, but one of the two terms is simply tossed out: here the material independent activity is the effect of the formal independent activity, so object-awareness becomes unintelligible, and we do not even understand how the philosopher manages to think of his own object (the reciprocity).

The essence of the dogmatic error is thus clear: in both cases the explanation of the reciprocity (between awareness and its object) is incompatible with the philosopher's reflection and thinkable only if we abstract from this reflection. In other words, a correct explanation of experience (the connection between an awareness and a world) must at the very least be compatible with philosophical reflection, which is also an object-awareness (in this case, the common awareness we are seeking to explain). Now because realism does not think of its own formal independent activity, it may imagine that experience (the awareness of objects) is correctly explained by causality alone. (If it reflected on its own operation, it would see that self-awareness, i.e., the existence for itself of passivity or the limit, is very much a necessary condition for its own reasoning.) Similarly, because idealism does not think of its own reflection on experience (its self-awareness of some object-awareness), it may believe that the operation of the imagination that "neutralizes the negative" (which reduces passivity to a least activity) is sufficient to explain experience. In both cases, therefore, the error is one of method, and Fichte's critique of dogmatism here repeats the essence of Kant's criticism.

2. The analysis of these two errors indicates how the philosophically correct view must make a synthetic composition of the duality of the independent activity, and how this is the only way to solve the problem of representation. The solution therefore is to posit that, just as experience presupposes the connection between self-awareness and object-awareness, philosophical reflection may neither be the effect just of the material independent activity (since in this case it would be pure "reflection," pure object-awareness, and in no way thinking), nor be reduced to a formal independent activity (for it possesses an object of reflection and cannot be reduced to pure self-awareness), which Fichte expresses in these terms: "That each (formal independent activity = the transition and the material independent activity = the ground X) should determine the other would mean ... that by the mere transition there is posited in the components that whereby transition can be made; and that by the positing of them as components, there is an immediate interplay between them. The transition is made possible by the fact of its occurrence; and it is possible only to the extent that it really does occur" (*SK*, 156).[27]

Here I shall merely sketch the results of this solution, for it is already possible to see the intimate connection between the critique of metaphysics (idealism and realism) and the notion of intersubjectivity. Let us note simply that a full resolution of the problem of representation—which thus appears as the central problem of theoretical philosophy—will again require making a synthesis of the reciprocity[28] by which experience (the reciprocity) will be defined as the indissoluble and reciprocal union of awareness and the world,[29] and finally the synthesis of the synthesis of independent activity and the synthesis of the reciprocity.[30] This last synthesis constitutes the first definitive venture outside of the dialectics of illusion, and for the first time points to the correct view of the question of representation. It posits the reciprocal and circular determination[31] of experience unified in the synthesis of the reciprocity and philosophical reflection on this experience unified in the synthesis of independent activity.

3. It is at this exact point, as Philonenko has shown, that the connection between the question of objectivity and that of intersubjectivity must be illuminated by reference to the notion of education. Discussing the proposition that the activity and the reciprocity reciprocally determine each other,[32] Philonenko has proposed the following reading: "The relation that realizes the synthetic unity of the independent activity and the relation as synthetic unity . . . is illustrated in the infinite movement of the teacher and the pupil, the latter in turn becoming a teacher of a pupil" (LH, 242). The teacher corresponds to the synthesis of the independent activity, for he is both the cause of the student's experience (the material independent activity) and a reflection of this experience (formal independent activity). Reciprocally, the pupil corresponds to the synthetic unity of the reciprocity, to the awareness plunged into the experience observed by the philosopher, so that we may unreservedly subscribe to this judgment by Philonenko: "Properly speaking, transcendental subjectivity is the knowledge of the subject by the subject that realizes itself in the relation of two awareness of which one knows the other the way the teacher knows the pupil. Of course, the pedagogical relation represents the genuine transcendental reflection of the subject in itself, which is realized in the recognition of the teacher and the pupil, of the philosopher and the nonphilosopher. In this connection the *Science of Knowledge* may be defined as a phenomenology of the understanding, for this movement brings about a convergence of the reflection of the teacher, who recognizes himself in his product, and that of the pupil who recognizes himself in his source" (LH, 242).[33]

2—From Intersubjectivity to the Philosophy of Rights

We should definitely clarify the notion of the "check" (*Anstoss*) to which this dialectics eventually leads us, by reference to this illustration of the solution to the problem of representation, just as we understand the transition from the *Science of Knowledge* to the Fichtean philosophy of rights which we shall now examine. Indeed, without analyzing further the synthesis of determinability, and just considering its results, we may say, no doubt simplifying Fichte's thought but without significantly distorting it, that it consists in (1) conceiving of the self as determinability that should be determined (further on, we shall see the ethical and political meaning of this formula which has so far been considered only in its theoretical aspect, i.e., as the solution to the problem of representation), and (2) referring to the not-self only as to a "check" (*Anstoss*), i.e., an originating impulse that, far from causally determining the self (in realist fashion) simply rouses it to determine itself. We should forego a dogmatically realist interpretation[34] of the "check" as Fichte conceives it, an interpretation in which the self once again inevitably reduces to passivity (which would take us back to the aporias of any theory of "reflection"). Here again, however, we should conceive of the reciprocity between the self and the *Anstoss:* "The self is by nature determinable only insofar as it posits itself as determinable" (*SK,* 190). So we should admit that "a mere check occurring without any concurrence from the positing self, could impose on the self the task of self-limitation" (*SK,* 190). Thus we must admit that "the check (unposited by the positing self) occurs to the self insofar as it is active, and is thus only a check insofar as there is activity in the self; its possibility is conditional upon the self's activity: no activity of the self, no check. Conversely, the activity of the self's own self-determining would be conditioned by the check; no check, no self-determination" (*SK,* 191). It is thus necessary to "compose," to synthesize the two terms: the activity of the self and the check, for, since one of the two is absent, the connection between self-awareness and object-awareness thus becomes unintelligible.

I think the following clarifies the significance of this necessity: if, as dogmatics would have it, the self was passively limited from the outside by an object, it follows that the self would be extremely limited (object-awareness), but that cannot be (self-awareness), because the limitation would by definition remain entirely outside the self: thus, representation (intentionality) would be completely inexplic-

117

able. Representation requires that the limitation be conscious—for the self, as it were—and hence not passive. We need, therefore, to understand how the external check may produce a representation (a synthesis of self-awareness and object-awareness) without our resorting to a causalist view: i.e., saying that the limit can exist for the self only if the self internalizes it, which can happen only through an *effort,* in the action of trying to get beyond this limit. Thus it is in a certain sense the self's infinity, meaning its constant effort to get beyond or to internalize every limit, which is the condition of its limitation for itself, a condition of the fact that the limitation provoked by the check on this potentially infinite activity (object-awareness) becomes conscious for the self (self-awareness), a conclusion Fichte expresses in these terms: "no infinity, no bounding; no bounding, no infinity; infinity and bounding are united in one and the same synthetic component" (*SK,* 192). To think of the self as limited, we must think it infinite: as the problem with dogmatic idealism shows, we cannot understand the self's self-limitation if we do not appeal to an external check, i.e., we must think of the self as infinite because its activity is not restricted in itself, but only by the limitation of a check that it tends to get beyond or to repel.

So we can solve the problem of representation by positing that theoretical reason is such because it is practical. At the level of theory, reason is led into a circle that critical idealism simply has the goal of bringing to light[35]: "It is contradictory to ask for a reality that remains after abstracting from all reason, for the person asking the question most probably also has reason, and is impelled by reason to ask this question, and desires a rational answer; hence, he has not been abstracting from reason. We can not go outside the domain of our reason ... and philosophy desires only that we shall become aware of this, and not believe that we have gone beyond it, when we are always within it" (*SR,* 62).

Thus it is practical awareness that conditions the theoretical awareness, which §1 of the *Science of Rights* is essentially intended to recall: "It is here maintained that the practical self is the self of original self-awareness; that a rational being perceives itself immediately only in willing, and that if it were not a practical being, it would not perceive itself, and hence would also not perceive the world, and that it would therefore not be an intelligence. Willing is the real essential character of reason; and representation, although in the philosopher's eyes, stands in reciprocal causality with willing—is posited as the accidental. That practical faculty is the innermost root of the self; to it everything else is attached, and with it connected" (*SR*, 36). It is thus from this angle that we should interpret the considerations in §1 concerning the analysis of the relations between will and representation.

The contradictory structure of the self positing itself as both finite and infinite, however, is for that very reason a structure of intentionality and is posited necessarily, for it is a precondition for theoretical awareness as a synthesis of self-awareness and object-awareness. This contradiction endlessly reproducing itself—for, by limiting itself, the self discovers that it is infinite, and vice versa—indissolubly unites intentionality and temporality since, in the circular composition of these steps, the imagination produces the three dimensions of time: "This interplay of the self, in and with itself, whereby it posits itself at once as finite and infinite—an interplay that consists, as it were, in self-conflict, and is self-reproducing, in that the self endeavors to unite the irreconcilable now attempting to receive the infinite in the form of the finite, now baffled, positing it again outside the latter, and in that very moment seeking once more to entertain it under the form of finitude—this is the power of *imagination*" (*SK*, 193).

Thus opened to temporality, the self is directly connected with a world. By positing itself as free, by ascribing to itself the spontaneous activity of free causality, it excludes everything that its action does not produce, as §2 of the *Science of Rights* highlights:

> Only the absolutely self-active, or practical, is posited as subjective, as belonging to the self, and by its limitation the self is restricted. Anything outside the domain of the absolutely self-active is posited, for the very reason that it lies beyond it, as not produced nor producible through the self's activity; hence, it is excluded from the domain of the self, and the self is excluded from its domain; and thus there arises a system of objects, i.e., a world that *exists independently of the self,* that is to say, of the practical self, which here stands for the self generally, and independently of which world *the self* (also, of course, the practical self, which determines its end) *exists likewise;* both of which, therefore, exist independently and externally of each other, and have both their separate existences (*SR*, 40–41).

In analyzing the preconditions of self-awareness, we have had to posit two elements: practical reason and, from it, the world: "The self must posit an external world, because it can posit itself in self-consciousness only as practical activity; and because, since it cannot posit anything but a limit, it must posit a limit to this practical activity" (*SR*, 41–42). We still have to see how, at the level of the doctrine of rights, objectivity (the connection of the awareness and the world) is possible only by reference to intersubjectivity, or, which amounts to the same thing, how we should, in the regressive analysis of the preconditions of self-awareness, get to intersubjectivity: Fichte does this in the third step of the first chapter of the *Science of Rights*, starting with proposition 3, according to which "the finite rational being cannot ascribe to itself a free causality in the sensory world without ascribing the same to others, and hence without likewise assuming other finite rational beings outside itself" (*SR*, 48).

In theorem 1, the positing of freedom and the world as conditions of self-awareness appears circular: we have seen that "a rational being cannot posit (perceive and comprehend) an object, without . . . ascribing causality to itself," but that, conversely, "it cannot ascribe causality to itself without positing some object to which that causality is directed" (*SR*, 48–49). Awareness thus seems inexplicable, for "all understanding is conditioned by the positing of causality of the rational being, and all causality is conditioned by a previous understanding of the same. Hence every possible moment of consciousness is conditioned by a previous moment of the same; and thus, in the explanation of the possibility of consciousness, consciousness is already presupposed. Consciousness can only be explained through a circle" (*SR*, 49).[36]

Thus, the only solution must be to assume that "the *subject's causality* is synthetically united with the object in one and the same time-moment" (*SR*, 51). And at this precise point we again encounter the structure of the solution already produced in the *Science of Knowledge:* only the idea of the "check," of the *Anstoss,* as not abolishing the self's activity—what's more, as possible only on condition of the self's infinite activity—works for the problem: the synthesis becomes possible "when we think of the subject as determined to determine itself; or when we think a request addressed to the subject to resolve on manifesting its causality," or again, "an external request that . . . must leave it, however, in full possession of its freedom of self-determination." (*SR*, 52, 53).

From the problem of objectivity, we were led to intersubjectivity as a precondition of theoretical awareness: it is clear that only another reasonable being can correspond to this definition of the "check," that only it can explain that a simple *Anstoss* is also an *Aufforderung,* an invitation to free action. Indeed, on the one hand, the check must not simply determine the subject causally (as it inevitably would do if the check were something simple), but it must leave the subject entirely free to act or not following this request; on the other hand, this request must be intelligible (since it must be understood, and, as such, to be the effect of an intention):

> This request to act is the content of the influence, and its ultimate aim is the free causality of the rational being to whom the request is addressed. This request does not determine or necessitate the rational being to act—as, in the conception of causality, the effect is necessitated by the cause—but merely takes this request as the occasion for determining itself to act. To do this, however, it must first have understood and comprehended the request, and this prior cognition of it is taken into account. Hence, the posited ground of the influence, or of the request addressed to the subject, must presuppose at least the possibility that the subject can understand and comprehend it, for otherwise its request would have no end in view at all. Its having such an end is conditioned by the understanding and freedom of the rational being to whom it is addressed. This ground must therefore necessarily have the conception of reason and freedom, and must therefore be itself a being capable of comprehending—i.e , an intelligence—, and since this too is impossible without freedom, it must be a free and hence a rational being, and must be posited as such (*SR*, 56–57).

Fichte illustrates this deduction of intersubjectivity as a precondition for self-awareness (therefore, as the ultimate solution to the problem of representation or the refutation of idealism) by the notion of education, which thus constitutes, even before rights, the first "model" of intersubjectivity: "The request on the rational being to manifest its free self-activity is what is called education" (*SR*, 61), and in this sense education is for the same reason as rights the "distinguishing characteristic of man,"[37] the ultimate condition of his humanity. The transition from the first model to the second, "to the legal relation in the strict sense, presents no great problems," for the idea of education already contains that of a reciprocal limitation of freedoms: to understand the request for self-determination, I must limit myself, for the initiator of the request can recognize me as a reasonable being only if I treat him as one;[38] the relation is reciprocal, for because the request is not a causal determination but a determination that leaves me free to determine myself, its initiator must also limit himself and treat me as a reasonable being: "The deduced relation between rational beings—namely, that each individual must restrict his freedom through the conception of the possibility of the other's freedom—is called the relation of legality, legal relation; and the formula given to it is called the Fundamental Principle of the Science of Rights. This relation has been deduced from the conception of the individual. . . . Again, the concept of the individual has been proven to be the condition of self-awareness" (*SR*, 78–79). And, I would add, because self-awareness in its freedom is precisely what dogmatic metaphysics, lost in the transcendental illusion and the aporias of the problem of representation, in no way manages to think through, the reciprocal connection that Fichte sees indissolubly uniting the deconstruction of metaphysics and political philosophy appears in all its clarity. It is by and in the critique of metaphysics, precisely when this critique takes the form of a "refutation of idealism,"[39] that authentic political thought becomes possible at the level of a theory of rights aiming to answer the Platonic question of the best regime; and, conversely, it is by and in the philosophy of rights that the critical solution of the problem of representation gets both its content and its meaning.

In the interplay of this reciprocal articulation, we may think of the "best regime" only as one that, in actualizing rights, opens up a public space of communication and intersubjectivity.

To see the meaning and scope of Fichte's answer to the central question of political philosophy, it may be helpful to compare Fichte's philosophy of rights with Kant's aesthetics: both combine an idea of intersubjectivity with a basically identical critique of dogmatic metaphysics.

When we consider Kant's procedure in the *Critique of Pure Reason* which makes possible reflection on aesthetic communication that is established in the *Critique of Judgment*, we can distinguish four stages:

1) First, the "Transcendental Aesthetic," the first part of the *Critique,* introduces an idea of finiteness expressed in the thesis that there is an a priori nonconceptual, i.e., the spatiotemporal forms in which particular existence is given us in intuition. As has sometimes been noted,[40] this conception of finiteness is diametrically opposed to the Cartesian conception that first posits the reality of the absolute (the existence of God) and after the fact conceives of finiteness as a lack (ignorance) in relation to the absolute. In Kant, on the other hand, finiteness comes first, so that what is relativized is the absolute, which "falls" from the rank of indubitable ontological reality to that of a simple "idea" or "point of view."

2) This reversal makes possible a critique of metaphysics that takes the form of a deconstruction of the "ontological argument" that

existence is deducible from (or reducible to) the concept. The definition of space and time as "pure intuitions" a priori guarantees that being cannot be the "predicate of a concept."

3) In Kant, however, the deconstruction of the illusions of metaphysics does not create—contrary, for example, to what takes place in Heidegger[41]—a tabula rasa. What metaphysics affirmatively posits as a theoretical truth is (at the aesthetic level, the only one that interests us here) simply transformed into a problematic requirement, a horizon of expectation or, in Kantian terms, a "principle of reflection." Thus, for example, the idea of a completed science, of a perfect coincidence between reality and rationality—an idea that metaphysics posits as genuinely objective, if not for us, then at least in itself or for God—, to wit: after deconstruction, the idea of a system[42] is preserved by virtue of a simple requirement, of a simple point of view that guides the understanding in the search for knowledge. So in this sense metaphysics retains a legitimate use, a "regulative role",[43] provided that, once again, we attribute no objective validity or truth to its concepts, but at the very most a meaning.[44] Deconstructed metaphysics continues to exist, therefore, by virtue of a horizon of expectation that is common to humanity: for example,[45] if it is illusory to assert the identity of the rational and the real, it is still legitimate to require the understanding to work indefinitely to approach this Idea. This idea thus plays the role of a horizon of theoretical expectation in relation to the progress of knowledge (understood as the progress of the rational over the real)—which however, remains radically contingent.

4) It is in relation to this horizon of expectation common to humanity that we may think of the space of aesthetic communication: the beautiful is basically a simple "trace" (symbol) of the idea of a system or, more precisely, the beautiful object is one that elicits agreement of sensibility (imagination) and of the understanding such as would be required to "present" or illustrate the idea of a system (the total identification of the real and the rational would indeed presuppose the perfect reconciliation of the sensibility and the concept).

In light of these few remarks, we can already state the essential features of aesthetic communication defined by the third *Critique*.

1) We first note that the space of this communication is open only on the basis of a critique of metaphysics, for it presupposes that the theoretical illusions are transformed into requirements or horizons of expectation: aesthetic pleasure essentially comes from the

contingency of meeting these requirements (in this case, that of the system), and this contingency, which presupposes that the proposition that the real is rational changes status, from an assertion to a simple viewpoint for reflection.

2) The aesthetic value thus "liberated" by the critique of dogmatisms therefore brings about a reconciliation between the particular (the sensibility) and the universal (the concept) which, far from being effected under the aegis of this concept, on the contrary results in the "free play of the faculties," from the particular to the universal; it is the real particular that by itself indicates the universal and freely reconciles itself with it.

3) For this reason, the aesthetic communication established among individuals around this "trace" of a deconstructed metaphysical idea that is the beautiful object appears as direct communication, as a source of immediate intersubjectivity: individuals are reconciled in it without the intermediary of a concept (as in scientific consensus) or a practical law (as in ethical consensus), as §39 of the third *Critique* stresses.[46]

4) In this sense, we may say the beautiful is the "distinguishing property of man" if, as the first pages of *Education* rather clearly indicate, man's essence is that he, unlike animals, is initially *nothing.* It may be on this point that the meaning of the connection between aesthetics and the critique of metaphysics shows up most clearly: man cannot be an element of a system; he is by definition what escapes the system, which, in other words, cannot be completely conceptualized.

5) This approach to man's humanity represents an incisive definition of illusion or ideology understood as the negation of the essence of man, a definition that traditional metaphysics is not alone in providing an illustration of.[47]

Reading of the first chapter of the *Science of Rights,* we easily see how these five characteristic points of Kant's articulation of aesthetics and the critique of metaphysics also apply to Fichte's political thought, or better, how Fichte thinks of political space as what in Kant was aesthetic space.[48] We first note that, as in Kant, the idea of intersubjectivity presupposes a critique of metaphysics that also essentially takes the form of a "refutation of idealism." We next note that— and this is what Gurvitch emphasizes—the goal of Fichte's legal thought is a synthesis of the particular and the universal (of individualism and universalism) and that this also leads to a theory of direct communication,[49] individuality being immediately connected to intersubjectivity as its precondition. Then rights, thought of as a process of reciprocal education (the reciprocal limitation being at the same time an inducement to self-determination), appears as "the distinguishing property of man."

In this sense, "only free, reciprocal causality on each other through conception and after conception, only this giving and receiving of knowledge, is the distinguishing characteristic of mankind, through which alone every person shows himself to be man" (*SR*, 61).

From the Critique of Historicism to the Critical Philosophy of History

The criticist critique of metaphysics, unlike Heidegger's or Strauss's, does not impugn subjectivity and humanism. Being critical, its decidedly more demanding aim is to protect the roots of modernity (reason and free will) from their possible dogmatic development which, contrary to what the partisans of the ancients think, this critique sees not as an acceptable achievement but as a betrayal.

To appreciate the pertinence of the criticist project—the only one explicitly to attempt to lay the foundations of a nonmetaphysical humanism—we need to examine two questions, both concerning the status of the nonhistoricist idea of history, to which, if it is to remain faithful to its aim, criticism should devote itself.

The first question concerns the relations between Hegelianism and criticism: Kant and Fichte—as well as everyone who followed in this tradition, from Hermann Cohen to Jürgen Habermas—dispute the ontological assumptions of historicism. Few, however, are unaware that Hegel's arguments against "the moral view of the world," which he believed was the essence of critical thought, are consequential, to say the least. Hegelianism presents a real challenge to critical thought: on an ethical and political level, it demands that critical thought defend itself against the accusation of "terrorism"; if the moral view of the world sees history as the actualization, through the free will of reasonable beings, of a universal ideal, how could this actualization—of which the French Revolution is the most striking exemplar—not be violent? Theoretically, on the other hand, what status should reason be granted in history if historicism (the assumption that the principle of reason is universally valid) is defeated? In other words, if we reject this principle, how can we avoid foundering in irrationalism?

The second question is the converse of the first: it concerns the relation between critical thought and phenomenology. From Heidegger's viewpoint, critical philosophy runs into two difficulties: one, ethical and political, links up, but only seemingly paradoxically, with the very one that Hegel thought he was disclosing: isn't subjectivity, conceived of as the reasonable will, inexorably fated to exercise tyranny over the world, a tyranny whose ultimate image, as we saw in the introduction, is the totalitarian terrorism of technology? For clearly different reasons, Hegel and Heidegger link up in the same critique of the moral view of the world: Hegel because he saw in it a deficiency of subjectivity (true subjectivity is not will but intelligence, for in seeing the perfect rationality of the real, intelligence makes the will's viewpoint superfluous and naive); Heidegger because he saw in it an excess of subjectivity (true subjectivity being the will, whose inevitable consequence is the will to power for the sake of power). The second—theoretical—difficulty faced by critical thought from Heidegger's viewpoint then becomes clear: doesn't the upholding, even though "critical," of a minimum of subjectivity imply a naively metaphysical idea of history, a view of events not as rooted in Being itself and hence mysterious (see Arendt) but as rooted in subjectivity, even if, once again, merely "residual" subjectivity?

The critical idea of history is thus forced to deal with a contradiction between three terms, *reason, will,* and *being,* when each in isolation forms the basis of a philosophy of history that is radically opposed to the other two:

- Reason, obviously, lays the foundations of a historicist philosophy in which mystery and free will have no place except as illusions (the determinism of the cunning of reason).
- The will lays the foundations of a philosophy of history, the moral view of the world, in which the principle of reason is violated, for indeterminacy (which is equivalent to Being) seems inconceivable.
- The history of Being removes historical events from these two "metaphysical" foundations, reason and will, thinking of them "with releasement" (*Gelassenheit*) as a "miracle of Being."

We cannot reduce critical thought to any one of these three positions: its essence is to start with facts, with what everyone agrees on (if only tacitly) in order to determine their preconditions; now the "fact" in this case is the seeming impossibility of thinking of history without reference to reason, will, and Being. Locking ourselves into one of these three positions is absurd. It is unworthy of a philosopher to want to "mix" them at the mercy of circumstances, by refusing, in the name of "good sense," to see their glaring contradictions. For its project to have meaning, critical thought thus must show how these three philosophies of history may even must, be articulated without contradiction. Only at this price can the critique of historicism cease to be a simple, negative, and sterile observation.[1]

NOTES

INTRODUCTION

1. I am thinking of Jürgen Habermas in Germany, but also of Raymond Aron in France who in 1978 did not hesitate to write an article called "Pour le progrès" in *Commentaire* 3. The fact that these two widely divergent writers both situate themselves in a Kantian tradition is not immaterial, as we shall perhaps understand better in what follows.

2. Max Horkheimer, "Traditional and Critical Theory," in *Critical Theory: Selected Essays*, trans. Matthew J. O'Connell et al. (New York: Continuum, 1982), 203.

3. Ibid., 210.

4. On the evolution of Critical Theory, see Luc Ferry and Alain Renaut, "Présentation," in Horkheimer, *Théorie critique*, trans. Ferry (Paris: Payot, 1978).

5. Horkheimer, "Traditional and Critical Theory," 204.

6. See Horkheimer, "Kritishche Theorie Gestern und Heute," in *Gesellschaft im Übergang* (Frankfurt: Fischer, 1972).

7. See ibid.

8. On the connection between Heideggerianism and German romanticism, see the excellent article by Robert Legros, "Romantisme et pensée de la finitude," *Cahiers du Centre d'Etudes phénoménologiques* 3–4 (1983).

9. Stanley Rosen stresses how much "Strauss himself was, in my opinion, and by his own admission . . decisively influenced by Heidegger," who eclipsed in his mind the image of Franz Rosenzweig.

10. See Martin Heidegger, "The Anaximander Fragment," in *Early Greek Thinking*, trans. David Farrell Krell and Frank A. Capuzzi (New York: Harper and Row, 1975).

11. See "OM," 26ff.

12. On Heidegger's analysis of the idea of system, see Renaut, "Système et histoire de l'Etre," *Les Etudes philosophiques* (April–June 1974).

13. See Ferry, "Stalinisme et historicisme," in *Les Interprétations du stalinisme*, ed. Evelyne Pisier (Paris: Presses Universitaires de France, 1983).

14. See Ferry, *Political Philosophy*, vol. 2 *The System of Philosophies of History* (forthcoming).

15. See Hannah Arendt, *The Human Condition* (Chicago: University of Chicago Press, 1958).

16. See Heidegger, *Nietzsche*, vol. 2, *The Eternal Recurrence of the Same*, trans. David Farrell Krell (New York: Harper and Row, 1984), 19ff.

17. Heidegger, preface to the French edition of *Wegmarken, Questions 1* (Paris: Gallimard, 1968).

18. See Heidegger, *Nietzsche,* passim. To discriminate between these two questions I write "being of being" with lowercase initial letters, and "Being" by itself with a capital letter.

19. Heidegger, preface to *Questions 1,* 9.

20. Heidegger, *Identity and Difference,* trans. Joan Stambaugh (New York: Harper and Row, 1969), 58.

21. See Heidegger, *Hegel's Concept of Experience* (New York: Octagon Books, 1983).

22. As the first thinker of a system, as Heidegger shows in his *Schelling.*

23. See Heidegger, "What Is Metaphysics?" in *Basic Writings: From "Being and Time" to "The Task of Thinking",* ed. David Farrell Krell (New York: Harper and Row, 1977).

24. Heidegger, *Identity and Difference,* p. 60.

25. Heidegger, introduction to "What Is Metaphysics?"

26. See Heidegger, "Zur Seinsfrage," *Wegmarken* (Frankfurt: Klostermann, 1977).

27. See Heidegger, *On Time and Being,* trans. Joan Stambaugh (New York: Harper and Row, 1972).

28. See Arendt, "Understanding and Politics," *Partisan Review* 20 (1953).

29. See Heidegger, "The Anaximander Fragment," 50–51.

30. See Heidegger, "Hegel und die Griechen," *Wegmarken.*

31. See Heidegger, *Nietzsche,* vol. 2. The lack of meaning here is clearly meant to echo the question of "the meaning of Being" raised in *Being and Time.*

32. See Heidegger, "What Is Metaphysics?"

33. See Heidegger, "The Anaximander Fragment."

34. Heidegger, "Hegel und die Griechen."

35. Ibid.

36. Heidegger, *Hegel's Concept of Experience,* 27.

37. Ibid. (Here Heidegger is explicitly using Hegel's vocabulary.)

38. Georg Wilhelm Friedrich Hegel, *Lectures on the History of Philosophy,* trans. E. S. Haldane and F. H. Simson (New York: Humanities Press, 1974).

39. Heidegger, "Hegel und die Griechen"

40. See Heidegger, *Zur Seinsfrage.*

41. See Heidegger, "What Is Metaphysics?"

42. Heidegger, "On the Essence of Truth," trans. John Sallis, in *Basic Writings,* 119.

43. On the error of translating this term by "open without withdrawal," see Renaut, "Vers la pensée du déclin," *Etudes philosophiques* 2 (1975).

44. Heidegger, "Hegel und die Griechen"

45. Ibid.

46. Notably in his *What Is a Thing?* trans. W. B Barton, Jr., and Vera Deutsch (Lanham, Md.: University Press of America, 1985).

47. See in *What Is a Thing?* the paragraph entitled "The Difference between the Greek Experience of Nature and That of Modern Times," 80–88.

48. Strauss's criticism of Heideggerianism as the height of historicism seems to me in this sense to be, in the best of cases, poor polemics.

49. See Ferry, "Stalinisme et historicisme."

50. See Ferry and Renaut, "D'un retour à Kant," *Ornicar* (1980), and Ferry, *Political Philosophy,* vol. 2.

51. Aristotle, *Physics*, trans. W. Charlton (Oxford: Oxford University Press, 1982), 4.208b, 4.211a.

52. Elisabeth Young-Bruehl, *Hannah Arendt: For Love of the World* (New Haven, Conn.: Yale University Press, 1982), 98.

53. From the introduction to the 1970 edition of Fichte's *Science of Rights:* "The French *le droit,* like the German *Recht(s),* means not only *right* in a political sense, but also *lawfulness* or *justice.*"—Trans.

54. See Ferry and Renaut, "Penser les droits de l'homme," *Esprit* (March 1983).

55. See Ferry, *Political Philosophy,* vol. 2.

56. Arendt, "Understanding and Politics."

57. See *Political Philosophy,* vol. 2, chap. 3.

58. See Heidegger, *Discourse on Thinking,* trans. John M. Anderson and E. Hans Freund (New York: Harper and Row, 1966).

59. See *Political Philosophy,* vol. 2, chap. 2, and chap. 6.

60. See Ferry, "Qu'est-ce qu'un critique de raison?" *Esprit* (April 1982).

61. See *LH.* I unreservedly follow Philonenko's interpretation.

PART 1, PREAMBLE

1. For an essay periodizing Strauss's thought, see Allan Bloom, "Leo Strauss: A True Philosopher," *Political Theory* 2, no. 4 (1974): 372–92.

2. Leo Strauss, *Political Philosophy: Six Essays by Leo Strauss,* ed. Hilail Gildin (Indianapolis: Pegasus/Bobbs-Merrill, 1975), 6. This collection includes two articles to which I shall be making frequent reference: "What Is Political Philosophy?" and "The Three Waves of Modernity". I thank Miguel Abensour for bringing these articles to my attention.

3. See also Strauss's "Political Philosophy and History," *Journal of the History of Ideas* 10 (1949): 30–50.

4. See, for example, the excellent review by Jacques Bouveresse, *Wittgenstein, la rime et la raison* (Paris: Minuit, 1973), 23, n. 4.

5. For a critique of Strauss's position that tries nevertheless to escape positivism, see Raymond Aron, *History, Truth, Liberty: Selected Writings,* ed. Franciszek Draus (Chicago: University of Chicago Press, 1985), chap. 12.

6. Pierre Manent, *Naissance de la politique moderne* (Paris: Payot, 1977), 8.

7. Strauss, "Political Philosophy and History," in *What Is Political Philosophy?* (Westport, Conn.: Greenwood, 1959), 60.

8. Concerning this methodology, see Ferry and Renaut, "Heidegger en question, essai de critique interne," *Revue de Metaphysique et de Morale* (1978).

9. This is the object of my *System of Philosophies of History,* vol. 2 of *Political Philosophy* (forthcoming).

CHAPTER 1

1. Strauss sees Kant as interpreting Rousseau to mean that "it is precisely because the processes ... not guided by human reflection are part of the providential order that their products are infinitely superior in wisdom to the products of reflection" (*NR,* 316).

2. Strauss's reading of Machiavelli is much more fine-grained in his major book about him.

3. On this point see also "PP," 47: "One must lower the standard in order to make probable, if not certain, the actualization of the right or desirable social order or in order to conquer chance."

4. "[T]he establishment of political society and even of the most desirable political society does not depend on chance, for chance can be conquered or corrupt matter can be transformed into incorrupt matter. There is a guarantee for the solution of the problem because a) the goal is lower, i.e., in harmony with what most men actually desire and b) chance can be conquered. The political problem becomes a technical problem" ("TW," 87).

5. See, for example, Martin Heidegger, *What Is a Thing?*" trans . W. B. Barton, Jr., and Vera Deutsch (Lanham, Md.: University Press of America, 1985), 76; or "WP."

6. On this topic, see also *NR*, 7, and "PP," 37, 55, and so on.

7. See also "PP," 42: "The power of man is much greater, and the power of nature and chance is correspondingly much smaller, than the ancients thought." This analysis of Protagoras's proposition is identical at every point with Heidegger's, as much in the *Nietzsche* as in the notes of "WP."

8. See also *NR*, 193–94.

9. For example, see "PP," 42: "Men are bad; they must be compelled to be good. But this compulsion must be the work of badness, of selfishness, of selfish passion."

10. See also *NR*, 207. On the connections between Machiavelli's thought and the Hegelian theory of the cunning of reason, see Claude Lefort, *Le Travail de l'oeuvre. Machiavel* (Paris: Gallimard, 1973), 110ff.

11. See also "PP," 51, as well as *NR*, chap. 5.

12. See also *NR*, 262.

13. "Rousseau takes it for granted that, in order to establish natural right, one must return to the state of nature. He accepts Hobbes's premise. Dismissing the natural right teaching of the ancient philosophers, he says that 'Hobbes has seen very well the defect of all modern definitions of natural right.' . . . [N]atural law must have its roots in principles which are anterior to reason, i.e., in passions which need not be specifically human" (*NR*, 266).

14. On this topic, see also *NR*, 266–71.

15. "Rousseau deviates from Hobbes because he accepts Hobbes's premise" (*NR*, 268).

16. For example, see "PP," 53.

17. See also *NR*, 271–72.

18. Contrary to what Strauss asserts, Rousseau does not admit this distinction "grudgingly." Rather, it forms the essence of his idea of freedom.

19. In this sense, it is difficult to understand how in "The Three Waves of Modernity" (90) Strauss can reduce the social order to the function of preservation. That amounts to confounding Rousseau's position with that of Hobbes and contravenes the very principles of Strauss's interpretation: if the good and just social order is defined as the nearest to perfect approximation to the state of nature, its end state may be merely the reproduction of freedom and in no way a guarantee of self-preservation. I will come back to this point further on.

20. On the emergence of this "existential" concept of freedom in Rousseau, Kant, and Fichte, see Alexis Philonenko's introduction to Kant , *Reflexions sur l'éducation,*

trans. Philonenko (Paris: Vrin, 1970). See also Ferry, *Political Philosophy*, vol. 2, *The System of Philosophies of History* (forthcoming), chap. 6.

21. On the circumstances of such a discovery and the birth of the philosophical interrogation, see *NR*, chap. 1.

22. I shall return further on to the difficulties that this description of the modern notion of the ought raises.

23. See also "PP," 39

24. See "PP," 32: "We may try to articulate the simple and unitary thought that expresses itself in the term *politeia* as follows: life is activity which is directed towards some goal; social life is an activity which is directed towards such a goal as can be pursued only by society . . ."

25. "We may also say [Socrates] viewed man in the light of the unchangeable ideas, i.e., of the fundamental and permanent problems. For to articulate the situation of man means to articulate man's openness to the whole This understanding of the situation of man which includes, then, the quest for cosmology rather than a solution to the cosmological problem, was the foundation of classical political philosophy" ("PP," 38).

26. "[T]he human soul is the only part of the whole which is open to the whole and therefore more akin to the whole than anything else" ("PP," 39).

27. "And Socrates was so far from being committed to a specific cosmology that his knowledge was knowledge of ignorance. Knowledge of ignorance is not ignorance. It is knowledge of the elusive character of the truth, of the whole" ("PP," 37–38).

28. "[T]here is no philosophy of history in classical political philosophy" ("PP," 55).

29. "The actualization of the best regime depends on the coming together, on the coincidence of, things which have a natural tendency to move away from each other (e.g., on the coincidence of philosophy and political power); it actualization depends therefore on chance" ("PP," 33). See also "TW," 85–87.

CHAPTER 2

1. This point is discussed in greater depth in my *System of Philosophies of History*, particularly in connection with the reception of the French Revolution by German philosophers. See *Political Philosophy*, vol. 2, *The System of Philosophies of History* (forthcoming).

2. In Kant the philosophy of history is not part of practical philosophy. It has the special status—which Strauss does not take into account—of a supposition of the faculty of judgment, which explains its being based essentially on the *Critique of Judgment*.

3. It would be quite easy to show how Strauss's representation of the gradual decline of modernity paradoxically ties in with certain aspects of Hegelianism: the same conception of the necessity of the succession of figures, the same representation of the successive interlinking of the questions that philosophers in turn "inherit," and the same idea that history is circular and must return to its origin.

4. See *Political Philosophy*, vol. 2, chap. 1.

5. See "TW," 90.

6. See *NR*, 276–81.

7. This is precisely what explains Fichte's critique of the seemingly strange presence of a theory of the cunning of reason in Kant. We should recall, however, that for

Kant this theory did not have the status of an objective truth but simply constituted a supposition, the historian's guiding thread. On this subject, see *System of Political Philosophy,* vol. 2.

8. Here I understand the term in its broadest sense as any philosophy in which the only motive of human action is, in the last analysis, self-interest or passion.

9. See Max Horkheimer, "The German Jews," in *Critique of Instrumental Reason,* trans. Matthew J. O'Connell and others (New York: Continuum, 1974), 101–18.

10. Particularly in the Marburg School and the Frankfurt School, but also, to some extent, in Hannah Arendt.

11. For example, see *NR,* 286: "the general will . . . means, for all practical purposes, the will of the legal majority."

12. See below, Part 2.

13. If perfection consists in "corresponding to its concept," man who is pure perfectibility can think of perfection only as an "idea."

14. See Diderot, *Encyclopedia,* addendum to 234.

15. See Strauss, *Persecution and the Art of Writing* (Glencoe, Ill.: The Free Press, 1952).

16. Thus Rousseau "inherited" the "problematic" of Hobbes who himself had "inherited" that of Machiavelli.

17. Until the 1950s, this was the standard interpretation in books about German idealism (with the notable exception of the work of Ernst Cassirer), of which the most representative is probably Richard Kroner's *Von Kant bis Hegel,* 2 vols. (Tubingen: J. C. B. Mohr, 1961).

18. See "PP," 24.

19. See *Political Philosophy,* vol. 2, Part 2.

20. See ibid.

21. Strauss's eminently Platonic idea about historicity seems to be unsuited to this project for yet another reason: it rests in a seemingly uncritical way on a "vision" of the truth as "recognition" or anamnesis. Thus it inevitably belongs to the Platonic tripartite scheme: classical thought functions as a Golden Age of political philosophy; next comes the time of forgetfulness and decline with the first wave of modernity; therefore, Strauss's political philosophy can see itself only as a return, a restoration of paridise lost. This tripartite structure, which is initially that of the Platonic theory of truth and which forms the ontological subbasement of his idea of time, is more actualized than it is contradicted in modernity. This is so true that its perfect elucidation coincides with the Hegelian completing of metaphysics, dialectics functioning precisely according to this trinity (*an sich, Dasein, für sich*). To my knowledge Fichte was the first and perhaps only philosopher to cast radical doubt on this metaphysical view of history in which the future may be merely a repetition of the past.

22. See *NR,* chap. 3.

23. See Pierre Manent, *Naissance de la politique moderne* (Paris: Payot, 1977), particularly pp. 9–11.

24. Ibid., p. 12.

25. Ibid.

26. Ibid., p. 11.

27. Except for attributing design to nature itself and thereby putting its effect within the framework of what could then rightly be called a theory of the "cunning of nature."

28. On this point, see Ferry, "De la critique de l'historicisme à la question du droit," in *Rejouer le politique* (Paris: Galilée, 1981).

29. See *Political Philosophy,* vol. 2, Part 2.

30. Georges Gurvitch, *L'Idée du droit social* (Paris: Sirey, 1932), p. 5ff.

31. See Ferry, "La distinction du droit et de l'éthique chez Fichte," in *Archives de philosophie du droit* (1981).

32. See *Political Philosophy,* vol. 2, introduction.

33. In the narrow sense of the expression, "German idealism" essentially designates "post-Kantian" philosophy, i.e., what goes from Kant to Hegel. We shall see that this expression should be extended to German philosophy from Leibniz to Hegel, for it was Leibniz who introduced the modern idea of a "system."

34. On the critiques of Kant's doctrine, see for example, Xavier Léon, *Fichte et son temps,* vol. 1 (Paris: 1922–27), 216–46, and Kroner, *Von Kant bis Hegel.* These critiques, particularly that of Freidrich Heinrich Jacobi, make the duality of foundation (the transcendental subject, the thing in itself) seem unsatisfactory in the *Critique,* just like the arbitrariness of a deduction of categories that remains "rhapsodical" (not truly deduced from a first principle).

35. See *ST.*

36. Here I am inspired by an article by Alain Renaut, "Système et histoire de l'Etre," *Les Etudes philosophiques* (April–June 1974): 245–64. This article is a critical study of Heidegger's *Schelling.*

37. Immanuel Kant, *Critique of Pure Reason,* trans. Norman Kemp Smith (London: Macmillan, 1929), 653.

38. Ibid. On the organic character of a system, see also Hegel, *Hegel's Philosophy of Right,* trans. T. M. Knox (New York: Oxford University Press, 1967).

39. Renaut, "Système et histoire de l'Etre", 243.

40. See also *ST,* 30–31.

41. The expression is not meant in its current sense. On the ontological meaning of the rise of mathematics in the modern era, see Heidegger, *What Is a Thing?* trans. W. B. Barton, Jr., and Vera Deutsch (Lanham, Md.: University Press of America, 1985).

42. This is basically the meaning of Leibniz's "principle of the best."

43. We clearly can see this in the definition of life given in the *Critique of Judgment,* to the extent that the two criteria of the living—reproduction and growth—are reduced by Kant to a third: self-production.

44. We shall see further on in what sense this "community" of projects is in fact less obvious than it seems.

45. Here again, we shall see that this seemingly common project assumes in reality a very different meaning, particularly depending on whether rationality is thought of as practical or as theoretical (in Fichte and in Hegel).

46. See the volume *Philosophies de l'Université, L'idéalisme allemand et la question de l'Université* (Paris: Payot, 1979), which contains writings by Schelling, Fichte, Schleiermacher, Humboldt, and Hegel. For a more detailed analysis of these texts, see the introduction (written in collaboration with A. Renaut and J.-P. Pesron) as well as Ursula Krautkrämer's *Staat und Erziehung* (Munich, 1979).

47. Directed by Minister Beyne to examine certain projects, Humboldt organized the University of Berlin inspired largely by Schleiermacher's plan.

48. See Heidegger, "What Is Metaphysics?" in *Basic Writings,* ed. David Farrell Krell (New York: Harper and Row, 1977), 96.

49. *On the Teaching of Philosophy in the Gymnasium* (1812) and *On the Teaching of Philosophy at the University* (1816).

50. No more than in the *Critique of Pure Reason.*

PART 2, PREAMBLE

1. We owe to Alexis Philonenko the first sensible, even sometimes brilliant interpretation of the whole of this text. After spending several years at the seminars of the
Center for Research on Kant and Fichte at the Ecole Normale Supérieure in Paris,
testing it against Fichte's writings, I have found no grounds for criticism of it. P.-Ph.
Druet also shares this view; see "Fichte et l'intersubjectivité, les thèses d'Alexis Philonenko," *Revue Philosophique de Louvain* (1973): 134–43. I was constantly stimulated
in what follows of this interpretation which I have attempted to the best of my abilities
to extend to the first chapter of Fichte's *Science of Rights.*

2. The following few pages repeat, without major modification, the very first pages
of chapter 2 of the second section my *Political Philosophy,* vol. 2, *The System of Philosophies of History* (forthcoming).

3. This well-known theme is elaborated, for example, in a letter to Niethammer in
1793 where we read that "Kant confined himself to indicating the truth, but neither
exposed it nor proved it."

4. It seems to me that in this sense the deduction of time and of matter in the
intuition does not at all have the "idealist" meaning that commentators before Philonenko attributed to it.

5. Immanuel Kant, *Critique of Pure Reason,* trans. Norman Kemp Smith (London:
Macmillan and Co., 1929). On the meaning of the concept of dialectics in Kant and
Fichte and on its evolution in Schelling and Hegel, see the masterful article by J. Rive-
laygue, "La Dialectique de Kant à Hegel," *Etudes philosophiques* (July–September
1978).

6. See *Sämtliche Werke,* 1:77. This runs counter to Hegel's interpretation.

7. On this point see the article on Fichte in Hegel's *Lectures on the History of
Philosophy* in which he regrets that "the deduction is finished at the second principle."

8. Thus this critique is valid as regards Schelling's first two texts. It is in other
respects interesting to note that this criticism is exactly the one Fichte addresses to
Schelling and Spinoza in his *Remarks on the Philosophy of Identity* showing in a text
that Hegel probably would have accepted how methodologically absurd it seemed to
him to take the absolute as the point of departure in philosophy. See Fichte, *Zur Dar-
stellung von Schellingsidentität, Nachgelassene Werke,* 11:371ff. Thus, this is a weighty
argument in favor of Philonenko's thesis.

9. See *LH,* chap. 5.

10. Hegel repeats this dialectic in his introduction to the *Phenomenology of Spirit.*

11. That is why Fichte finds Spinoza's philosophy absurd, for everything in it happens as though it were "between two others": between a "subject" not-self and an
"object" not-self; see *SK,* 101.

12. We have already seen how the positing of the first principle as illusory implies
the positing of the not-self, for it leaves free the reflection that "deduces" it from the
same logical construction as the one that allowed for the positing of the absolute self.
It is also clear, however, that the not-self presupposes the self or that, as Fichte says,
"the possibility of counterpositing itself presupposes the identity of consciousness."
The reasoning may be quite simple here: not-A presupposes A; now, A is identical to
the proposition "A = A." This last proposition (consistent with the first principle) is
itself based on the proposition "self = self" from which the absolute self is deduced:
"Hence even the transition from positing to counterpositing is possible only through
the identity of the self" (*SK,* 103).

13. Fichte formulates it this way (my comments in parentheses): "if I = I, every-thing is posited that is posited in the self. But now the second principle is supposed to be posited (because it has the same logical presuppositions as those we admitted to posit first) in the self (because the absolute self contains everything), and also not to be posited therein (because it is precisely a not-self). Thus *I* does not = I, but rather self = not-self, and not-self = self"(*SK*, 107).

14. The first formulation of the third principle, which posits the absolute self as substrate, is nevertheless still illusory and provides only the framework of the solution: see *LH*, 256, n. 39.

15. See *LH*, 254ff. (in which Philonenko demonstrates the aptness of this compari-son by showing how the thesis and the synthesis are reversible).

16. On the philosophical level, this issue is that of the relation between the prin-ciple of the identity of indiscernibles and the principle of continuity; see *LH*, 275ff.

17. This is the property of the whole criticist critique of reason: See the interview mentioned earlier, "Qu'est-ce qu'une critique de la raison?" *Esprit* (April 1982).

CHAPTER 3

1. For an analysis of this process, see *LH*, 182ff.

2. "The one defect is that you thought profoundly, but didn't think your own thought itself," quoted by Philonenko, *LH*, 204.

3. We find a detailed analysis of this question in Martial Gueroult, *La Philosophie transcendentale de Salomon Maïmon* (Paris: Alcan, 1929), 59ff; see Xavier Léon, *Fichte et son temps*, vol. 1 (Paris: Armand Colin, 1922–27), 230, and particularly Jacques Rive-laygue, "La Dialectique de Kant à Hegel," *Etudes Philosophiques* (July–September 1978).

4. See Salomon Maimon, *Versuch über die Transcendentalphilosophie. Mit einem Anhang über die symbolische Erkenntnis* (Berlin: Christian Vos, 1790, 419–20.

5. Maimon, *Versuch.*

6. Maimon, *Philosophisches Wörterbuch, oder Beleuchtung der wichtigsten Gegen-stände de Philosophie* (Berlin, 1791), 169.

7. By the "Transcendental Aesthetic" which implies the infinite resistance of the given.

8. Immanuel Kant, *Critique of Pure Reason*, trans. Norman Kemp Smith (London: Macmillan and Co., 1929), 202. The inspiration for this commentary on the relation between Maimon and Kant came from Rivelaygue's "La Dialectique de Kant à Hegel." See also *LH*, 282.

9. This proof rests on the thesis that there is no empty time, a thesis that forms the basis of the argumentation in all the proofs of Kant's "Analytic of Principles."

10. *Critique of Pure Reason*, 201–2. See *LH*, 282.

11. The degree N is produced by an integral that results from the subject's activity. But it is still true that each intermediate degree of awareness between O and N has a content that is not produced by this subject.

12. Maimon, *Versuch*, 620.

13. This comment was inspired by a lecture by Rivelaygue at the Collège de Philo-sophie in 1980.

14. See *LH*, 204.

15. On the concept of the doctrine of science, see Fichte, *Über den Begriff der Wissenschaftslehre, Sämtliche Werke*, 7:364.

16. On this "philosophical attitude," see Max Horkheimer, "Zum Rationalismusstreit in der gegenwärtigen Philosophie," in *Kristische Theorie*, vol. 1 (Frankfurt: Fischer, 1968).

17. The project of Hegel's *Phenomenology of Spirit* seems to be the only one in metaphysics that takes Fichte's critique into account and accepts the challenge: in a certain sense, all dialectics in Hegel's *Phenomenology* is an attempt to explain the status of the finite subject relative to the absolute.

18. See *ND*, and also Joachim Ritter, *Hegel und die Französische Revolution* (Cologne: Westdeutscher, 1965), 41, n. 23.

19. Alexis Philonenko has quite rightly pointed out that only the *Critique of Judgment* develops the idea of intersubjectivity. While in the *Critique of Pure Reason* and the *Critique of Practical Reason* communication is indirect, because it goes, in the first case, through the mediation of the concept and, in the second case, through the mediation of the moral law, the *Critique of Judgment* deals with a "direct communication of man with man, of that mode of communication where man encounters man without making a detour through the object (concept) or the law" (introduction to Kant, *Critique de la faculté de juger*, trans. Philonenko [Paris: Vrin, 1968], 11).

20. See *Critique of Pure Reason*.

21. Philonenko, introduction to *Critique de la faculte de juger*, 15.

22. Philonenko, *Théorie et praxis*, 147.

23. It appears that the theorists of the Frankfurt School knew too little of Fichte to recognize him as one of their forerunners. Only Kant played this role.

24. Horkheimer, "Traditional and Critical Theory," in *Critical Theory: Selected Essays*, trans. Matthew J. O'Connell et al. (New York: Continuum, 1982).

25. Max Horkheimer, "Kritische Theorie gestern und heute," *Gesellschaft im Übergang* (Frankfurt: Fischer, 1972).

26. See the critique of positivism by Horkheimer in "Das Problem der Wahrheit" and "Zum Rationalismusstreit," in *Kritische Theorie*.

27. *Traditional Theory and Critical Theory*.

28. "The vast majority of men have a common interest in the rational organization of society," we read in Horkheimer, "Zum Rationalismusstreit."

29. See Ferry and Renaut, "Présentation" in Horkheimer, *Théorie critique*, trans. Ferry (Paris: Payot, 1978), 9–41. On the effect of the reference to Marx in *Kritische Theorie*, see also Ferry and Renaut, "M. Horkheimer et l'idéalisme allemand," *Archives de Philosophie* (April 1982).

30. Martin Jay, *The Dialectical Imagination: A History of the Frankfurt School and the Institute of Social Research* (London: Heinemann, 1973), 258–59.

31. We find an excellent description of Horkheimer's and Adorno's "administered world" in Horkheimer, "Kritische Theorie Gestern und Heute."

32. I do not of course subscribe to this analysis. The only thing that interests me here is its critical structure.

33. For example, Heidegger just confirms this failure by his critique of subjectivity, paradoxically agreeing with the result, central to Adorno, of the Hegelian system. In his *Negative Dialectics* Adorno repeats the idea of the ontological difference (the nonidentity of the concept and being), although without accepting the "implications" that Heidegger drew from it about the liquidation of the subject. Here again, therefore,

Adorno seems close to Kant and Fichte despite the reference to materialism that mortgages his thought in other respects.

34. Hence Adorno's severe though extremely attentive critique of Heidegger.

35. Here Adorno is discussing the repetition by Marx and Engels, those "atheistic Hegelians," of the theory of the cunning of reason. The relation to criticism is clear. We thus see how Adorno thinks the illusion of the cunning of reason is in a way concretely realized in what he writes in "After Auschwitz" (see *ND*, 361ff.). It follows that this realization is not a verification, but, on the contrary, the height of illusion: "Absolute negativity is in plain sight and has ceased to surprise anyone. Fear used to be tied to the *principium individuationis* of self-preservation, and that principle, by its own consistency, abolishes itself. What the sadists in the camps foretold their victims, 'Tomorrow you'll be wiggling skyward as smoke from this chimney,' bespeaks the indifference of each individual life that is the direction of history" (*ND*, 362).

36. This essential difference—for it leads to historicism—does not, however, affect the character of the necessity that Adorno thought defined the metaphysical illusion, as is shown by the text quoted earlier. The persistence of this form of materialism in Adorno (a form he borrowed from Alfred Sohn-Rethel) is evidently a source of problems that Jürgen Habermas gave a good analysis of in *Theory and Practice*, trans. John Viertel (Boston: Beacon Press, 1973) and also in *Philosophical-political Profiles*, trans. Frederick G. Lawrence (Cambridge, Mass.: MIT Press, 1983). It seems indeed difficult to legitimize the resistance of the finite subject by anchoring it in a figure of "historically" transcended subjectivity (that of the individual bourgeois). We can solve this problem only by renouncing the "materialist" idea of a situation and that of a historical genesis of categories. See Ferry, "La Raison ou ses marges," *Débat* 4 (1980).

CHAPTER 4

1. See Georges Gurvitch, *L'Idée du droit social* (Paris: Sirey, 1932), 95ff.

2. Ibid., 409.

3. See Fichte, *Sämtliche Werke* (Berlin, 1965), 3:286; and Luc Ferry, "La Distinction du droit and de l'éthique dans la pensée du jeune Fichte," in *Archives de Philosophie du droit* (1981).

4. See *L'Idée du droit social*, 407ff.

5. See also: "the conception of law is the conception of a relation between rational beings. Hence it exists only when such beings are thought of in relation to one another" (*SR*, 81).

6. Fichte, "Lectures on the Vocation of the Scholar" in *Fichte: Early Philosophical Writings*, ed. and trans. Daniel Breazeale (Ithaca N.Y.: Cornell University Press, 1988), 155. Fichte adds that this question must be answered for a "fundamental science of natural rights to be possible."

7. Ibid., 154.

8. Ibid.

9. See Kant, *Critique of Judgment*, §64.

10. "Vocation of the Scholar," 155.

11. Ibid., 154.

12. See Ferry, *Political Philosophy*, vol. 2, *The System of Philosophies of History* (forthcoming), chap. 6.

13. Opposed, if only in that the law often allows acts that morality may well censure. See *SR*, 80–81.

14. It is this philosophy of history whose preconditions I attempt to indicate in the second part of my *Political Philosophy*, vol. 2.

15. Alexis Philonenko has published a paragraph-by-paragraph commentary on this text. See *LH*.

16. See *SK*, 143ff.

17. Fichte introduces the concept of independent activity to resolve the conflict between idealism and realism, but at this level its meaning remains undetermined. ("Activity of this sort we shall term for the moment *independent* activity, until we are better acquainted with it" [*SK*, 141].) Only in the application of this solution to causality and substantiality can the meaning of this idea become clear, as it were, by reference to the history of philosophy (to Spinoza and Leibniz).

18. Philonenko has provided a "translation"—extremely valuable for shedding light on this text—of Fichte's concepts into Spinoza's terminology:

> If we consider Spinozism, it will be easy to identify the concepts corresponding to passivity, dependent activity, and the independent activity of the not-self. Passivity is the affection. The act-passivity relation, which includes the dependent activity of the not-self, is the "*natura naturata*." ... The causal nexus between some modes and others explains how from passivity in the mode—for example, of the finite human mind—we can determine the activity corresponding to this passivity.... The *natura naturans* remains to be defined. We can define it in these terms: "God insofar as he is considered a free case"—"*Deus quatenus ut causa libera consideratur.*" We will parse this definition as follows": "*Deus quatenus*"—the independent activity in relation of the act-passivity relation that it grounds—"*ut causa libera*"—the independent activity, the real reason of the act-passivity relation is merely the cause of this relation so this relation is uniquely qualitative—"*consideratur*"—it is in reflection that the independent activity is asserted as the foundation of the act-passivity relation." (*LH*, 211)

19. "[P]assivity as such, and in respect of its quality, is to be nothing other than activity; though in respect of quantity it must be a lesser activity than the totality" (*SK*, 148).

20. Here again, we may refer to Philonenko's invaluable guide on the translation into Leibniz's terminology of this analysis of dogmatic idealism; see *LH*, 213.

21. See *SK*, 152.

22. See *LH*, 206.

23. It is indeed the case that "this activity of transference . . . is attributable *to the self*" (*SK*, 152).

24. See *SK*, 154–55.

25. For the analysis of this text we may refer to the work of Philonenko (*LH*, 228ff.) who sheds important light on its almost insuperable obscurities, notably by translating Fichte's concepts into Spinozistic and Leibnizian terms.

26. Let me suggest beforehand that Philonenko's reading of the *Science of Knowledge* sheds light on the idea of independent activity by proposing to interpret it using the concept of education: this concept appears particularly appropriate for illustrating the idea of a synthesis between the material independent activity conceived as the foundation of the relation between awareness and its object and the formal independent activity understood as reflection about this relation: education is both the "cause"

of the pupil's experience and at the same time reflection about this experience. Starting with realism, Philonenko explains his interpretation this way:

> If we consider Spinozism materialistic, we will be persuaded to call experience the act-passivity relation; it indicates *natura naturata*, i.e., the causal nexus connecting the mode's passivity with the not-self's activity that determines it. . . . The independent activity corresponds, on the one hand, to the causality of the substance of *natura naturans* . . . and, on the other hand, to the philosopher's reflection about the act-passivity relation and its foundation. . . . The idea of an independent activity as synthetic unity thus must have a twofold character: on the one hand, it must determine the act-passivity relation as Spinozistic substance; on the other hand, it must correspond to the philosopher's reflection. These two features appear incompatible: what does it mean to speak of a synthesis of the material independent activity and the formal independent activity?
>
> It appears to me that we can express this synthesis using a capital idea of Fichte: the idea of education. In Fichte, the educator is defined by two features. On the one hand, he carries out an action on another consciousness; in this sense he appears first as a not-self source of an affection. . . . On the other hand . . . he does some reflection. . . . We may say that the broadest sense of the idea of independent activity as synthetic unity is Fichte's notion of educator. (*LH*, 229–30)

This interpretation seems to me necessary for an understanding of this obscure idea of the independent activity. Further on, we shall see how this reading is largely confirmed by chapter 1 of the *Science of Rights*.

27. [Parenthetical remarks are the author's.]

28. See *SK*, 156–57.

29. This synthesis answers in this sense the question asked in the fourth paralogism of the *Critique of Pure Reason,* for it refutes the idealism and skepticism resulting from it by showing how awareness is necessarily awareness of a world and the world necessarily a world for awareness.

30. See *SK*, 157. It should be noted that the result of this last synthesis will later be applied to causality and substantiality. Despite their importance and extreme difficulty (notably for the latter), these developments do not essentially change the solution to the problem of representation sketched in this text.

31. See *SK*, 159.

32. "The activity determining the form of the interplay determines everything that emerges therein, and conversely, everything that emerges in the interplay determines it" (*SK*, 158).

33. It follows that in its connection to the theory of objectivity this structure of educative thought again is better illustrated in the "deduction of representation" or "pragmatic history of the human mind (see *SK*, 194ff) as Philonenko shows (*LH*, 304ff.). In it we see how, from a simple "check," objectivity is constructed through sensation, imagination, and the understanding, and how, with judgment and reason, intersubjectivity appears as the precondition of objectivity (the not-self requiring to be conceived as another self so that the idea of a determination to self-determination gets all its meaning).

34. On this interpretation, see *SK*, 189–90.

35. Theoretically, the analysis of the problem of representation leads us only to posit the necessity of a reconciliation of idealism and realism without our being really able to understand the meaning of this reconciliation, as Fichte himself stresses: "Hence the real question at issue between realism and idealism is as to which road is

to be taken in explaining [re]presentation. It will become evident that in the theoretical part of our *Science of Knowledge* this question remains completely unanswered; that is, it is answered by saying: Both roads are correct; under a certain condition we are obliged to take the one, and under the opposite condition we must take the other; and by this, then, all human, that is, all finite reason is thrown into conflict with itself, and embroiled in a circle" (*SK*, 147).

36. See also the reformulation of this circle, *SR*, 51.

37. "All individuals must be educated to be men; otherwise, they would not be men" (*SR*, 61).

38. See *SR*, 68–69, 82–83.

39. And here Fichte is carrying out Kant's project.

40. This is obviously the case in Heidegger, but also in Ernst Cassirer (see for example, his review of Heidegger's book on Kant in *Kantstudien,* number 36). M. Alquié has supported the converse thesis; see *La Critique kantienne de la métaphysique* (Paris: Presses Universitaires de France, 1968).

41. We mean that Heidegger leaves no *legitimate* use for metaphysics, so that the very idea of a *Critique of Judgment* becomes impossible, for it assumes that we agree on a minimum of legitimacy (in meaning, if not in truth) to deconstructed metaphysics in order to make it a "horizon of aesthetic expectation" or a "principle of reflection." This "radicalness" of Heidegger's deconstruction seems to be a source of exceptional difficulties.

42. See *Critique of Judgment.*

43. See Kant's appendix to the "Transcendental Dialectic."

44. Here is where Kant's theory of symbolism comes in.

45. See *Critique of Judgment.*

46. In his introduction to a French edition of the *Critique of Judgment,* Philonenko rightly draws the reader's attention to the importance of this point; see *Critique de la faculté de juger,* trans. Philonenko (Paris: Vrin, 1968).

47. It is from there that a critique of the project that, very often, motivates the "human sciences" would seem to me possible.

48. To my knowledge Philonenko is the only interpreter to have realized the scope of this rapprochement which he briefly suggests in his introduction to the *Third Critique* (see *Critique de la faculté de juger,* 15). Note that on this point, Fichte announces—but also "anticipates"—the thought of Jürgen Habermas.

49. See *SR*, 68–69, 78.

CONCLUSION

1. It is from this perspective that I have tried, in the next volume in this series, to formulate the preconditions for this articulation.

INDEX

INDEX